TIME MANAGEMENT FOR WRITERS

TIME MANAGEMENT FOR WRITERS

Ted Schwarz

Writer's Digest Books

Cincinnati, Ohio

Time Management for Writers. Copyright © 1988 by Ted Schwarz.
Printed and bound in the United States of America. All rights reserved.
No part of this book may be reproduced in any form or by any
electronic or mechanical means including information storage and
· retrieval systems without permission in writing from the publisher,
except by a reviewer, who may quote brief passages in a review.
Published by Writer's Digest Books, an imprint of F&W Publications,
Inc., 1507 Dana Ave., Cincinnati, Ohio 45207. First edition.

92 91 90 89 88   5 4 3 2 1

Library of Congress Cataloging-in-Publication Data

Schwarz, Ted, 1945-
    Time management for writers / Ted Schwarz.
        p.   cm.
    Includes index.
    ISBN 0-89879-309-2 : $10.95
    1. Authors—Time management. 2. Authorship—Technique.
    I. Title.
    PN145.S28 1988
808'.02—dc19   88-5710
                                                                    CIP

Design by Joan Jacobus

Contents

Introduction

I am not organized. Let's get that fact settled right at the start. My desk is littered with papers, books, computer disks, and cassette tapes of interviews. I have two telephones teetering precariously on stacks of notebooks, a cat asleep on my computer monitor, and a dog asleep on even more papers scattered about the floor. When my wife and I put our house up for sale so we could move East, the real estate agent politely tried to tell me that my place was too messy to show in its present state. Thus this book is not going to tell you how to turn your life into a flawlessly efficient mini-bureaucracy of designer file drawers filled with research material and work in progress. You will not learn to be a perfect parent, a flawless spouse, or to time every aspect of your life so that you are never late, never tired, and always looking your best.

But while I am not organized by nature, I am a writer who produces what, even to me, is a disgustingly large volume of work each year. I seldom am involved with fewer than a half dozen major books, twenty or more magazine articles and short stories, radio shows, and at least one movie. I also travel, am active in my community, and spend as much time as possible with my wife. I have learned to identify the time I have available, the priorities that matter to me, and other factors that affect the process of living. I have learned to manage my time.

This is not to say that I have enough time each day to do all the things I would like to do. The one problem with being a writer, whether a beginner or a professional, is that you never have enough time. If you work full time at something other than your writing, you are lucky if you can grab five or ten minutes during the day to think about your field of interest. Any actual work must be accomplished before or after your job, a situation that often means very early morning or very late at night.

If you work part time, it often seems that just as your words are beginning to flow on the paper, it is time to return to that other job. You become frustrated with your dependence upon the part-time income because you know it is hindering your development as a writer.

And if you do not hold a job outside your home, chances are you are reading this because your responsibilities do not allow you the freedom you seek. You are probably in the position of caring for your children, an elderly parent, or a spouse entitled to large chunks of your time, attention, and emotional energy. If you have the luxury of enough money to write without outside work and have none of these restrictions, your friends and family will probably not take your writing seriously. They are likely to view your writing as a meaningless hobby, suggesting that you always have the time to run errands, volunteer to assist your child's teacher, make appointments to other people's convenience, and generally function as the community "go-fer."

I remember when I finally began selling enough of my

work so that I could freelance. My office was in my home. I arose early because that was when I was most creative. And if I took a break to rest during the day, I would often work into the evening. I had deadlines, query letters to get out, and local publishing contacts to pursue. But this reality was so different from the nine-to-five type of routine familiar to others, I regularly encountered a subtle prejudice and lack of understanding.

For example, the dental hygienist was scheduling an appointment to clean my teeth. She knew I was a professional writer and I was quite proud of the fact that I could pay the bills by then without an outside job. But the hygienist quickly deflated my ego by saying, "We can schedule you any time because you don't work."

A friend, after struggling as an editor for a magazine she hated, finally made enough article sales to quit her job. She longed for endless hours of writing without interruption but her friends, seeing that she was "no longer working," began inviting her to lunch each day. When she told them she was busy, they became angry with her for being such a self-centered snob that she would not admit that she was unemployed. (She was earning $2,000 a month writing at the time.) Even her soon-to-be-ex-boyfriend, a man who worked nights, began stopping by to cheer her up.

At best, the person who stays home to write is viewed as having a "hobby" to be taken up or put down at the whim of others. It is not serious work. It is something tolerated, usually with a bemused smile and a gentle pat on the head, much as you'd give a small child scribbling with crayons. (Until my mother saw my name on *The New York Times* best seller list, she was waiting for me to get a "real" job.)

Yet the reality for all of us who write is that we are *driven* to pursue this field. We love what we do, we constantly strive to improve, and we agonize over the time constraints that are unchangeable in our lives. The knowledge that we can make more efficient use of our time pleases us, yet most writers have no idea how to take advantage of these precious extra minutes.

This book will thus address two of the most important concerns for any writer. The first is time management—learning to evaluate the time you can spend writing, then utilizing it to the fullest. And the second is maximizing research—taking the results of that well-managed time and expanding the markets to which you are selling. But before we explore these issues, the following quiz will help you determine how badly you need to consider more efficient time management.

Can You Benefit From Better Time Management?

1. Do you find yourself watching television or listening to the radio because you can't find enough time to write?

2. Do you find yourself constantly harassed by last-minute chores that seem to eat away at your free time?

3. Do you find yourself saying, "If only I had half an hour (an hour, a day, a weekend, or some other specific time period), I could accomplish a lot of writing?"

4. If you listed everything you're committed to do every week—cleaning, laundry, home maintenance, shopping, cooking, personal (church, PTA) etc.—and realistically estimated how long each would take, would these routine commitments take all your "spare" time and more besides, so that you put off some and ignore others?

5. If your answer to question 4 is "yes," do you still consider each chore as necessary, even though you keep putting it off? Do you carry such chores over from week to week rather than admit some could be skipped completely without personal suffering or a sense of loss? Do you try to do all chores yourself rather than delegating them to other members of your family?

6. Do you really need as much sleeping time as you routinely get, to feel alert and fully rested when you wake up?

7. Do you feel obligated to talk to someone on the phone regardless of the time or circumstances?

8. Do you feel that you must see one task to completion before starting another, even if there are periods when you find yourself to be nonproductive?

9. Do you tell yourself that you will be ready to write as soon as you can buy an electric typewriter, a word processor, or a computer?

10. Do you accept invitations to parties and events you neither wish nor need to attend because you feel that the experience might help your writing?

11. Do you feel put upon by others because you routinely agree to do something for them they could just as easily do for themselves?

12. Do you tell yourself that you will start writing as soon as you convert a room or special space into a permanent work area?

HOW TO SCORE

Give yourself one point for each "yes" answer. If you have one to three "yeses," you are doing a better-than-average job of time management. The tips in this book will help, but you are to be congratulated for what you have accomplished.

Four to five "yes" answers show that you have made an effort to manage your time but are having problems. More than five "yeses" means that you have been keeping yourself from being productive as a writer. This book's time management advice will prove essential to your part-time or full-time career as a writer.

One

DECIDE ON YOUR PURPOSE

Your writing can take many forms. You can write books, magazine articles, short stories, screenplays, or newspaper features. You can concentrate in one area because you find it most enjoyable, or you can vary your work, perhaps writing novels and nonfiction books, or short stories and screenplays, or whatever combination you enjoy. Generally, the greater the variety of your work, the more productive you will become. Irving Wallace, for example, is the author of novels, nonfiction works, magazine articles, and even such unusual research projects as *The People's Almanac* that he coauthored with his son and daughter. In contrast, the work of the equally skilled Arthur Hailey is completed one project at a time. While Wallace seems to always have a new project in bookstores or on magazine racks, Hailey seldom has more than one book every three years or longer.

Generally, the more you write in a variety of areas, the easier it is to utilize your time most effectively. You can be researching for one project, interviewing for a second, and writing a third. As you become tired of one, another is fresh in your mind. The more radically different your efforts, the easier it is to feel rejuvenated as you move from a project where you have lost your perspective and enthusiasm to one where you are excited about the work and make the best writing decisions.

Of course there are exceptions. The late mystery writer John Creasy (aka Jeremy York, Gordon Ashe, and a variety of pen names) wrote hundreds of mysteries, switching among characters and settings instead of types of work. Georges Simenon, the French mystery writer, also concentrates in one genre. But the important point is that they work on several projects at once.

Should you follow the examples of these professionals? That depends. What is the purpose of your writing? What are your goals for your work? How easy is it for you to stay with one field, or to switch concentration from one subject to another?

In general, it is best to write in the same manner that you would work in other fields of endeavor. A normal workday in an office, a factory, school, or other place of employment is constantly changing. You are doing paperwork, having meetings, selling, teaching, tuning up an engine, making change for a customer, or whatever. To do otherwise would become boring. You would begin slowing your pace. You would talk of "burnout" just as writers talk of "writer's block."

By doing several projects at once, you will always find yourself fresh. You will work on one project for an hour or two, then get tired of it and find that you are fresh for something quite different. Or you might work on a project for several weeks, then suddenly decide that you never want to see it again. By the time you become disenchanted with the alternate work, you find that you are so fresh for the first that you wonder why you ever took a break from it. In fact, most "prolific" professionals may actually be slower writers than those who turn out less work. They just juggle several projects simultaneously so that they are always working. Deadlines will vary so that they are not unduly pressured and they may spend years researching one project part time while writing others. But they always have more than one project in the works.

Knowing this reality, you have to make several decisions. First, what do you want to write? Short stories can be written fairly quickly. Once you have the idea in your head, you will be writing in whatever time you are able to spend, polishing the work with each new draft until it is ready to submit. Seasonal work must be submitted from three months to six months in advance. If you are the type who can only think about a season during that period of the year, then you will have to hold the work in your files for from six months to nine months before submission.

Articles also require about six months' lead time. They also require research in most instances, unless you are discussing a field in which you are an expert, or writing humor or a personal essay. The research may involve time in the library, a visit to a museum or other location, and/or interviews with acknowledged experts. Whatever the case, you must do the research before beginning the writing so your time involved in producing the work will increase proportionately.

Whether you are writing articles or short stories, you will traditionally be paid in one of two ways—on acceptance or on publication. The latter is risky because publication of a timeless story or article may be many months—or even a year or more—later or it may never be published at all. Payment on acceptance usually means within thirty days of acceptance. With magazines offering this extremely fair method of payment, you will learn their schedule and come to be able to count on a regular check for your articles and short fiction. You will be able to plan your income based on the frequency of your sales to such markets.

Book sales result in a much greater lead time. If you have never sold a novel before, or if you have sold a novel or two but are not staying with the same genre, you are probably going to have to complete the entire book before offering it in the marketplace. Writers are frequently told that they can sell a novel based on four chapters and an outline, a reality that does occur for some. Unfortunately, so many new novelists have developed good ideas and strong leads they were unable to bring to a satisfactory ending, that most publishers are unwilling to take a chance. They want to see the completed book.

A SEASONAL BUSINESS

A writer interested in selling a novel should be aware that publishing has its seasons. Between Thanksgiving and the second week in January, there is generally a casual attitude towards new acquisitions. People are taking vacations, having holiday parties, taking a day or two off for Christmas shopping. Attempting to get a decision on a particular project during this period is extremely difficult. Likewise, July and August are usually major vacation times. If a book is not so timely or so much in demand that it must be purchased or it will be lost to another house, it's hard for a writer to get a quick, definitive "yes" or "no." Another one to two weeks are lost in August during the international book fair in Frankfurt, Germany when many of the top decision-makers are out of the country. Thus a book completed during certain periods of the year is likely to languish in the editorial offices, awaiting the return of enough people to make a decision.

What does all this mean? Simply, that a novel may take a year or more to sell from the time you first start to write it. The brilliance of the writing, the thoroughness of your outline, and possibly even your publishing track record may account for little.

A nonfiction book is slightly easier to sell. A solid outline and four or five chapters usually will be enough to obtain a contract. A writer with a track record in the field may be able to submit even less and still sell the book. The periods when publishing decisions are least likely to be made are consistent for all types of books, but your lead time from idea to sale is often no more than three to six months. In addition, the average nonfiction book has a more predictable market than most novels. The advance you will receive is thus likely to be higher than for a novel.

Television movie scripts and feature films fall somewhere between the two. There are seasons when the networks are open to ideas and periods when they are more concerned with the development of already purchased products. There are production companies that purchase scripts and ideas all year 'round and those whose decisions are made shortly before they might have to pitch a new idea to the networks. In theory, feature films are purchased throughout the year, but in practice, smaller companies may buy most frequently between release seasons (generally summer and near the Christmas season, though now companies are experimenting with January and April "off season" releases with heavy marketing). Even worse, your work may just be optioned, in which you are paid a small fee for the right to develop your idea or script. An option may be for six months or a year, usually with renewable option clauses included so the project can be tied up, with an appropriate fee paid, for up to two years. It is not unusual to have a $100,000 contract for the rights to a script, yet never receive more than $5,000 in option money before the project is dropped. However, after an option expires, you can resell the same idea or script to someone else, assuming it is not dated.

Television and the movies are cyclical as well. If you have written a brilliant script that does not fit the current cycle of Westerns, "disease of the week" plots, teen exploitation pictures, fantasy movies, "slasher" films, or whatever is currently popular, wait six months to a year and your work may suddenly be saleable. Thus a television or film project may take two or three years of marketing before it sells.

Newspaper feature writing is another outlet. Depending upon the type of work you are producing—column, feature, news, etc.—your lead time as a freelancer will range from a minimum of twenty-four hours or less to a maximum of six weeks. The pay comes more quickly than with magazine writing, but frequently is far less.

What does all this mean to you? If you have a burning desire to write in one particular field, and many people do, recognize your lead time and plan to earn a living at some other job until you have a few sales to your credit. Even the most successful first-time novelist will still have a year or more from the time he writes the opening sentence until money predictably comes in. Others may have to wait until their second novel, or even longer. The prolific John Creasy wrote more than seventy mystery novels before making his first sale. Elmore Leonard was selling novels for several years before being "discovered" with best-seller status and Hollywood contracts.

By contrast, the article writer can often begin making a sizeable supplemental income right away. This is especially true in larger communities where you can combine freelancing for national publications with work for local and regional newspapers, magazines, and public relations agencies.

If your purpose is to earn your living as a writer and you enjoy all types of writing, then you should plan on mixing articles that are readily sold, short stories that may take longer to find a market but still pay fairly quickly, and longer-term projects that may eventually pay quite well. The latter would include both books and scripts, areas that can only become full-time sources of income after you have made a few sales and found a market (or markets) for larger work.

If your purpose is to write novels or biographies or screenplays or some similar specific, lengthy work, then you must recognize that at least at the beginning, you will be earning your living in some other field. Your time-management program will be based on finding time in addition to a regular job instead of phasing out that regular job to find increasing time for writing, something that is desirable only with fairly predictable paychecks for your work.

Thus the first rule is to know your purpose in writing. Then accept this reality, adjusting your life accordingly. You may phase into more frequent writing sessions if your goals are such that you can generate regular income fairly quickly. Or you may have to accept the fact that you will always be a little frustrated about not having as much time as you would like for writing the novels that may each take a year to sell.

MULTIPLE PIECES FROM ONE IDEA

There are two types of marketing approaches that will increase your effective use of writing time. One is called *simultaneous submission*. The other involves developing a variety of articles and/or stories from a single idea.

There are two types of simultaneous submissions. One involves the submission of query letters and the other involves the submission of completed articles and short stories. There is never anything wrong with submitting identical query letters to competing and noncompeting magazines alike. The more timely your submission, the more important it is to be certain all possible markets are contacted.

By contrast, submitting finished work to competing magazines will likely create a problem for you. This is an ethical rather than a legal matter as will be explained more fully in chapter 5.

Editors want a unique product, not something the reader may have seen elsewhere, regardless of the publication.

The one exception is fiction. A short story may be sold in the United States and to noncompeting magazines overseas (England, Australia, etc.) providing the publishers are aware of what you are doing and do not have overlapping circulations.

The reasons for the taboo are many. Basically, a magazine requires satisfied readers in order to sell advertising space. Since it is the advertising sales that generate the profits for a publication, and since advertising rates are based on circulation, anything that may discourage readers is taboo. What this means is that if an editor even suspects that a reader will avoid an article or short story because he or she has seen it elsewhere, that material will not be purchased. Few people read every article and story in every magazine they buy, but they will at least skim most of the material for something to catch their fancy. The more frequently they ignore an article or short story, the more likely they are to think they can live without the purchase. They will pick up a rival magazine that has nothing they have seen before, helping to reduce the circulation of one magazine and boosting the circulation of the other. Since magazines already have circulation problems when rivals appear on the stands (*Playboy* dominated the men's magazine field until *Penthouse* and *Hustler* came on the market; *Woman's Day*, *Family Circle*, *Ladies' Home Journal* and *McCall's* compete for the same readers; etc.), buying multiple submissions works against them. (I'll discuss simultaneous submissions and multiple marketing tactics in more detail in chapter 5.)

By contrast, you can take one idea and develop it into a number of different projects. This is "multiple marketing." Most familiar is the book that is sold to the movies, then adapted for the screen. There is also the short story character who evolves into the subject of a book. Novelist Lawrence Block developed a burglar who was the delightfully irreverent hero of a short story. He evolved into the main character of such books as *Burglars Can't Be Choosers*, *Burglar in the Closet*, and others. Eventually "he" became a "she" in a comedy/mystery feature film starring actress Whoopi Goldberg.

More common, and more easily controlled, is the book ideas used to spin off magazine articles. For example, when I researched a book on the history of coinage, I produced a number of articles based on completed chapters. Though quite different from the chapters, the articles were related to the same period of history and many of the same people. They sold to hobby magazines in the United States and England. A reverse of the process was an article I wrote for *Wom-*

an's Day on a boy who received a liver transplant at the University of Pittsburgh Children's Hospital. That article evolved into the book *A Gift of Life* (with Parichehr Yomtoob), published by St. Martin's Press. At this writing, plans are to obtain a movie option on the story as well.

Q. David Bowers is a writer/publisher/businessman in the hobby field. He will periodically write a series of articles about an area of special interest, such as stamp collecting, then package those articles as a book.

Likewise, by changing focus on the same theme, you can develop magazine articles in this way. For example, I wrote an article for professional photographers on how to relocate their studios when the neighborhood changes or they need to expand. This evolved into an article on how to relocate an optometrist's office, another on how to relocate a medical office, and several others, each aimed for a specific trade journal. The concepts for all the articles were the same and the business information is a constant. But each article was written as a unique entity and aimed for a specific audience. The businesses mentioned were noncompeting and the articles, while containing many of the same basic facts, varied according to the needs and interests of the reader. In this instance, my pay for the original article was $125. My total income from writing several uniquely different articles following the same original research was almost $2,000. Since the research often takes longer than the writing, and since the articles could be written one after the other without further interviews, my eventual per-hour earnings were much higher than if I had researched and written one article, then researched and written a totally different one.

MULTIPLE-MARKETING AN IDEA

1. What is your subject? If it's business-related, what other businesses might have an interest? If it's science-related, consider both children's and adult publications. For market ideas, study the current *Writer's Market*, as well as magazines that

might be concerned with the impact of the specific topic. Whatever the field, consider magazines that might relate to any individuals who are the subjects (e.g., teens, the elderly, etc.), businesses, general interest publications, hobby magazines, and so on.

2. List competing and noncompeting magazines in all fields that might have an interest in some aspect of your topic, article, or book.

3. What articles could you produce with your existing research or a limited amount of supplemental research? For which of the markets on your list will they be appropriate?

4. Query noncompeting magazines concerning the relevant topics. Query competing magazines only if you can develop radically different articles on the general subject matter, articles that will in no way seem related to readers of both publications.

BAD HABITS/GOOD HABITS

Several bad habits may prevent you from utilizing your time as effectively as you need to. The first is assuming that writers have a minimum amount of time during which they can work. Erma Bombeck began her career as a newspaper columnist in Dayton, Ohio, when her children were young and needed extensive attention and her husband was an educator. She grabbed five minutes here and there while handling the myriad household tasks she has humorously recounted in what is now one of the most successful syndicated humor columns in the United States.

Frederic W. Rosen, the author of three books, dozens of articles, and an adjunct professor of writing, decided to freelance while working as a magazine editor for a company that required frequent travel. Sometimes he could grab ten minutes in an evening for his own freelancing. At other times he had the luxury of a half hour or an hour. The time was so minimal and so irregular that he seriously considered not bothering. He could have watched television, read a book, lingered over the newspaper. He knew that "real" writers only work when they have longer periods of time, yet he ignored his fears and used what few minutes he could to write. Within a year he was able to make enough sales to quit his job and become a full-time professional writer.

I followed a similar approach while working full time in a hospital's research department. Periodically I would have a five-minute break during which I would write short humor and make notes concerning ideas for longer work. I had another hour or two to write most evenings if I wasn't too tired. By the time I left the hospital's employ, I was freelancing comedy for NBC Radio, had a newspaper humor column, and was writing history articles. The money was somewhat limited, but I had a professional base.

The point of all this is: Do not assume that you have to have a set period of time or you can't work. Take advantage of spare moments, whenever and wherever they occur. Keep a pen and small notebook or a microcassette tape recorder with you at all times. If you have a long commute to your job, carry a tape recorder that can be used for dictating ideas, listening to interviews, lectures and/or talking books that might relate to your writing, and otherwise being productive.

Another bad habit is trying to write what others have told you will sell instead of what you enjoy. Many times a bookstore owner or other well-meaning person, upon learning that you are trying to become a writer, will tell you the "only" way to go. This might be writing a romance or a horror novel or a how-to book. The person will quote some article he's read, or the vague "friend of a friend." Should you follow the advice, you will find that the subject does not interest you and you begin finding ways to avoid working.

Instead, write what you enjoy reading or about subjects that interest you. Working this way, you will find yourself looking forward to every spare minute you can steal from your otherwise busy day. You will rewrite as much as necessary. You will polish your work and master your craft. Not only will your time be used most efficiently, you will always be working to the limits of your ability because your writing will be fun.

Be cautious about taking too many courses in writing and spending too much time reading about it. There are two reasons to study writing through magazines, classes, and correspondence courses. One is to learn how to improve. The other is to avoid facing blank paper or an empty computer screen.

I read every issue of *Writer's Digest*. I read *Publishers Weekly*. I keep up with the Hollywood trade journals important to my work and I always encourage writing students to at least read *Writer's Digest* regardless of their level of expertise. Everyone, whether beginner or professional, needs to maintain an awareness of both the business he is in and concepts and ideas that may help improve his writing. You and I are no exceptions.

The problem comes when the writing courses and the books on writing become ways to avoid the work. You will recognize this yourself if you find yourself saying such things as: "I don't know enough to write," "I'll start after I take Professor Expert's course on literature," or "Since most writers have college degrees, I at least should improve my education before I try to put words on paper." Or any of the other dozen comments that might be made to justify such thinking. If this sounds familiar, then it is time you put down the writing course catalogs and started to write.

Earlier you took a quiz concerning your need for time management. One of the questions concerned whether or not you have ever made a list of your necessary chores.

One bad habit many writers have is trying to go in all directions at once. Instead of looking at their week and planning ahead, they respond to crisis after crisis. They grocery shop on Saturday without a list, hoping they will remember everything, then have to pick up milk on Tuesday, bread on Wednesday, hamburger on Friday.

Likewise there are other distractions, such as the need to buy more typing paper, pens, ribbons, or similar supplies. There are friends who want to go to lunch or just have a friendly chat.

In many instances, what you are doing is simply not planning ahead. There are certain chores which must be completed in the course of a week. By listing them, then planning for the most efficient use of your time, you may save yourself hours for writing.

For example, map out the places where you shop, work, attend school, chauffeur your children, or whatever else is your particular circumstance. Which facilities are grouped near each other? Which require the most driving? Which require the least? Often you will find that just by changing your habits so that you handle several of your weekly errands at the same time, you come out ahead. In my own case, I group a library run with trips to the post office and any related shopping, such as purchasing audiocassettes for recording interviews. The three facilities are near at hand, but before I started working more intelligently, I would go to the post office one day, the library another, and waste time on a third getting the cassettes I knew I would need. Likewise, when other types of shopping have to be done, I try to pick a location that is also near one of the supermarkets where my wife and I like to shop. One trip handles everything whereas before I was adding an additional hour commuting time. It seems like a little thing, but sometimes that extra hour has come in handy for completing a short story I am submitting on speculation where I cannot afford to use normal work time.

Another bad habit is using writing time to prepare for writing. Leave routine chores like sharpening pencils, changing the ribbon in your printer, looking through *Writer's Market*, and opening reference books to appropriate pages for when you are tired. For me, this means just before going to bed, though the specific time does not matter. You do not want to waste the writing time when you are likely to feel most creative handling nothing but busywork. Get in the habit of so preparing yourself and your writing area that you can begin writing the moment you sit down.

Finally, and this may sound a little odd in a time-management book, adopt an attitude of self-respect. If you have never sold any of your work, perhaps are only now even trying to sell, you may find that you have a tendency to belittle your efforts. Your spouse may joke about your "hobby." Your children, if you have any, may feel that they can interrupt you because you are "only" at the typewriter. Your parents may think your actions are "cute" or that you are wasting your time. And because you have yet to sell, you may become discouraged and decide that perhaps they are right. You may then find yourself not taking advantage of the time that you do have because you don't respect your efforts.

The truth is that all writers start slowly. Scott Turow, whose novel *Presumed Innocent* became a financially successful best seller, was hailed as a brilliant "first novelist." The impression of the publicity was that he sat down to write a book, did so, and became an overnight success. In reality, Turow had been writing for several years, though with only modest success. He wrote the book in longhand on the commuter train. He, like you, had faced the same time pressures and family concerns. He undoubtedly had identical stress, but when you read about him, you begin to think that he was one of the blessed. He was someone who knew, along with all those around him, that fame would be instant.

Everyone starts with the same frustrations, the same time constraints, the same comments of disbelief from family and friends. Respect yourself! Writing is what you want to do, so get in the habit of doing it. You may feel discouraged. You may be frustrated because you get so little support from your family. But so long as you can retain your self-respect, knowing that you are developing your writing skills and working towards publishing goals, you will not waste what time you have. This may mean rising early or going to bed late. This may mean demanding an hour during the day or the weekend when you are not to be disturbed for anything other than a true disaster. But maintain your self-respect so that you do not waste what precious time you have.

DETERMINING POTENTIAL WRITING TIME

It is important to understand all possible drains on your writing time. The following questions will help you put your time in perspective. The list is divided into categories, but you should answer all the questions that relate to your personal circumstances.

YOUR TIME COMMITMENTS

1. Which days and hours are committed to working each week? If you are a full-time student, list your school commitments, including the minimum hours of study you must put in to maintain the grade average you need. If you are a student who works, list the combination of work and school hours.

2. List the activities with which you are involved each week that you will not change. These may include church or synagogue attendance, volunteer work, health club activity, etc.

3. List the minimum hours of sleep you need to be adequately rested to work effectively each week.

4. List the time you spend doing essential chores such as grocery shopping, preparing meals, showering, etc., each week.

5. List the time you spend commuting to and from your job each week.

Total the hours and fractions of an hour for questions 1 through 5 and subtract that figure from 168, the total hours available to you in a week. This is the number of hours available for all other activities, including writing. Next take this figure and subtract the number you listed in question 5 from the total. This will be the time you can spend in surroundings most conducive to any type of writing. How you use your commuting time will vary with how you commute. A car driver is limited to listening to audiotapes, dictating notes into a tape recorder and thinking through plots. A writer who takes the bus will usually be able to do little more than either read or think. The same is true for most rail commuters except on trains, where it is frequently possible to write, either in a notebook or on a laptop computer.

SPOUSE OR OTHER LIVE-IN RELATIONSHIP

When you live with another adult, there will be certain periods of time that overlap. Cooking and eating time will usually be the same. You are likely to sleep at the same time. Whatever the case in your life, do not concern yourself with the hours that are shared that have been listed in the first section. Instead, look at the relationship and see what additional time demands this second person puts on you and the time demands you choose to accept.

For example, is the person elderly and/or in need of special care? This will be a time factor to record. Is there a regular time you wish to set aside for intimacy, whether that means making love, going for walks together, or just talking without interruption? Determine this and add it to your list. Whatever additional time involvement the relationship demands should be included.

Finally, subtract this figure from the total you achieved in questions 1-4 because your time is now subsequently reduced by this amount. Again you can use this total and subtract the number in question 5 from it in order to determine the time where you can work in controlled surroundings.

CHILDREN

Repeat the above process to determine how much time will be spent with your children. This time your considerations will vary with the age of the child, whether or not he or she is old enough to take public transportation, and the activities to which the child is committed. There will also be periods of attention that the child needs in order to receive adequate nurturing and emotional bonding.

ANALYZING THE RESULTS

The number of hours per week that you have available for writing will always be a little frustrating. This is because you enjoy the work so much that anything that keeps you from it can seem like a nuisance. However, you can make some changes with the knowledge you have gained.

For example, the biggest drain everyone experiences is from the busywork of daily life. Going to work, to the grocery store, taking children to music lessons, to visit friends, to the library, cleaning house, fixing meals, and all the myriad other activities seem the most trying and sometimes needless drains you can experience. Fortunately there are ways around them.

TWO

MAKING THE TIME TO WRITE

Your first concern is setting aside a time and place to write. The place can be anywhere you can leave your materials and keep returning.

For example, Sue Downey, a freelance writer who works for a variety of publications in southern Arizona, made a broom closet her first "office." She added two shelves, one at a height designed to be comfortable when she was working at her typewriter and the other, somewhat higher, to hold various reference books. She had a folding chair and forced herself to ignore the other items stored in the closet. It was cramped, a little frustrating, but it was hers. Equally important, her husband and son knew that when they came into the house and saw the broom closet door open, she was in her office and not to be disturbed. Only after several years and many sales was she able to build a small room onto the house, a room used exclusively for her work.

Some writers use a desk in the corner of the living room. Others use a kitchen table while their children are in school. Still others use a portion of their bedroom. My first apartment was a tiny efficiency that had the kitchen separated by an odd unit that was part closet, part hanging light, part board that stuck out at such an angle that it could be used as a table for eating. My bed was a fold-down couch; I had two chairs and some sort of coffee table just large enough to hold a television set and some books. I turned the eating area into my office (it held the typewriter, paper, a dictionary, and the telephone) and ate on a tiny folding table that was purchased at a Salvation Army Thrift Store.

Seldom are you fortunate enough to have an ideal location such as an entire extra room to yourself when you first start. What is important is that you have a specific area you can return to every chance you get.

Just as you plan a place for writing at home, plan for writing when you are away from home. Carry two pens with you at all times, along with a small notebook or pad of paper for jotting down ideas. Or you might prefer a small cassette recorder. Whatever the case, keep the tools for writing handy at all times so you can let your mind roam free, always knowing that whatever concepts you create will not be lost by the time you return home.

SAYING NO TO OUTSIDE DEMANDS

Professional writers often have trouble saying no to outside demands. Cynthia Scanlon, a prolific magazine writer who works in the bedroom of her home, notes that friends frequently invite her out to lunch while she's working. "You don't work so you can go out anytime" is their attitude, and they are hurt when she refuses to join them. Yet she knows that writing must be a business and the time when she can work cannot be wasted.

You may be just starting as a writer but you need to adopt the proper attitude. Try to think of your writing time as a part-time job, even if you are only able to grab ten or fifteen minutes at any given moment. You would not want to hurt your employer by leaving work to chat with friends, taking long lunch hours, or otherwise deviating from what you are supposed to be doing. Do not hurt yourself by engaging in such activities.

Now determine the real time you have to write. Take into consideration coffee breaks, lunch breaks, and commuting time if you work, as well as time between classes if you go to school.

When planning do not look for large blocks of time. The reality is that you will never have enough time. The more you write, the more ideas you generate, the more you will want to write, and the more frustrated you will become.

For me, I have found that it is best to work *all* the time instead of an isolated hour or two. For example, when I still had to hold a full-time office job, we were given two coffee breaks and a lunch break. The lunch break was taken at the same time by everyone in my department. We all ate together and it would have been rude to do otherwise. However, we always took our coffee breaks alone and grabbed any time possible. Thus I used those breaks to develop ideas, think about plots, write a few jokes, or whatever else I could in that short time. I carried a small notebook with me in which to jot down ideas.

Obviously I could not always shift my thoughts easily from work to my writing. There were many days when I was frustrated rather than effective. Yet I produced enough work or developed enough ideas so that I was more effective during the time I had allotted for writing at the end of the day.

A bus driver friend of mine sold his first work to *Playboy* and *Esquire* working on his portable typewriter during turn-around breaks. It is not how much time you have but *how you use it* that makes the difference.

Look at the time you have at home and analyze what is important. There has to be a certain level of cleanliness in our lives, yet where is it written that a lawn must be mowed before your neighbor complains that her son got lost delivering the paper from the sidewalk to your front door? Is there any reason to worry about the grass unless you step on your front porch and hear drumbeats and see smoke signals coming from the dense underbrush? When I owned a home with a lawn, I found that I gained an extra period for writing by mowing the lawn every ten days instead of once a week. I was in a neighborhood where most people took pride in their yards and expected others to do the same, yet adding an additional three days between mowings did not upset anyone.

Likewise, while bathrooms and kitchens need cleaning for health reasons, other parts of the house can get a little dusty. A child's room that looks like an "after" picture for a first-strike nuclear attack can best be treated by hanging an "Out of Order" sign on the closed door. And meals do not have to take several hours to prepare according to Cordon Bleu standards every day. If the food is nutritious and edible, anyone who complains can take over the chore of cooking.

Analyze your interpersonal involvement with your family. One writing student of mine was a young mother who was concerned about spending time with her children. However, she realized that she wasted an hour a day while watching "Sesame Street" and "Mr. Rogers' Neighborhood" with her children. They weren't listening to her. There was no parent/child interaction. They were both sitting glued to their seats, watching the set. She simply rearranged her actions, taking that hour for writing, then being with the children when they could truly interact. A family that talks together, reads aloud together, goes for walks together is a family that is being nurtured. A family that sits and stares at the television set is not being enriched. Thus that may be the ideal time for you to be involved with writing.

Likewise, find ways to work while doing other tasks. Do you have a dog who needs walking? Try working through plot twists or deciding a chapter's structure while following the dog at the other end of the leash.

I have found that it is best to make a chart of each day of a typical week. Make note of all your activities from the time you awaken until you go to sleep. Then notice which segments you can "steal" through slight rearrangement.

It may also help to budget alternative activities from time to time. For example, my wife and I both love movies and are fortunate in living near a public library that has literally thousands of videocassettes for loan. When I am working intensely on deadline, I try to spend my evenings writing. However, because I am keeping long, pressured hours, there are nights when I am too tired to think. Those are the nights we borrow or rent a videocassette and watch a movie. Not only does this relax us both, but because I write for the film industry and it is my business to keep up on current productions, I never feel guilty about the time spent.

Other writers choose to read reference books when they are too tired to write. Or they read genre fiction related to the type of work they are producing. And some even have the wisdom to take a nap.

GUARDING YOUR TIME

Once you have a place to write and know your potential time availability, you must reduce distractions to a minimum. As I mentioned earlier, treat your writing time as a part-time job regardless of how close you might or might not be to selling your work.

Unplug your telephone or buy an answering machine, if you can afford one, for the time when you are writing. If you have circumstances where telephone calls may be important, answer the telephone but refuse to speak with anyone who is not of immediate concern. Call people back or ask them to call you at a certain time. Refusing to talk a few times will get the message across to friends who eventually will start calling at a more convenient time. Just remember to say "no" even when they tell you that what they have to say will just take a minute. Too much time is lost in this manner.

Have your family handle chores that are realistic for them during this period. The chores might be setting the table or doing the dishes. They might include running errands or even having family shopping needs divided among several people when you go to a shopping center.

As I mentioned at the end of chapter 1, respect yourself, respect what you are trying to do, and let no one interrupt you needlessly. Asserting yourself will be difficult when you have yet to make a sale and it is hard to see your writing as a business. But writing is a growth skill. The more you write, the better you become. I have been selling for more than twenty-five years and I always try to make my current work the best of which I am capable and better than what has come before it. I like to say that I am only as good as my next work. Thus writing time, whether you are an established professional or just entering the field, must be treated with respect.

ORGANIZING YOUR WRITING

Alex Haley, the author of such bestsellers as *The Autobiography of Malcolm X* and *Roots*, and the *Playboy* magazine interviews (he developed the concept), is extremely slow and methodical. *Roots* evolved over a period of seven years, according to the author.

Isaac Asimov has written several hundred books and more articles than he has probably counted. He may skip from a science fiction novel to a mystery to Bible commentary to a science article for an airline magazine. He is at the other extreme where several projects must be organized at any given time and numerous submissions are in the marketplace.

Most likely you are somewhere in between. You are writing more than one project in order to stay fresh, but not so many that you need a computer just to track the range of ideas you are developing.

There are two aspects to organization. The first is the gathering of materials, reference works, etc. that you will need; the second is finding a place to store them.

The types of reference works you should have will vary with the type of writing you do. As a general rule, I feel that every writer must have a dictionary that is current and as complete as he can afford. A new, unabridged dictionary is ideal but expensive. Almost as good, and cheaper to update, is the so-called college type published by several companies. Just remember that words change constantly, some becoming acceptable through usage and others developing as society changes. You may think that only scientific jargon evolves, but try to find "break dancing" in a dictionary published ten or twenty years ago. That fad may be out of style today, but if you are writing about the early 1980s, it is one of many terms related to popular culture, some of which you will have to look up.

A recent dictionary-style thesaurus is also of tremendous help. I say dictionary-style thesaurus because it is the easiest type to use. Other types have an elaborate cross-referencing system that can be confusing and takes needless time.

Optional extras are specialized reference works related to your particular writing. For example, my desk includes a regularly updated dictionary of American slang terms, a dictionary of medical terms, also regularly updated, a dictionary of American biography, a Bible dictionary, and some general guides to collectibles. These personal necessities reflect my specialized writing needs.

I consider three other reference works to be necessities. One is the current *Writer's Market* which I feel every writer should obtain, no matter what type of work he does. I also maintain the current *Fiction Writer's Market* and *Photographer's Market*. Some writers may need *Songwriter's Market* or some other specialized guide.

You don't have to subscribe to periodicals if your library has them. The only one I consider a necessity for writers is *Writer's Digest*. Others you may wish to read regularly, depending upon your type of writing, will include other periodicals for writers as well as such specialized trade journals as

Publishers Weekly, the daily or weekly *Variety, Broadcasting* magazine, *Hollywood Reporter*, and *Editor & Publisher*.

One often-overlooked reference is the telephone directory. A telephone directory is essential for local business information. You will want the Yellow Pages and, if separate, a "business-to-business" Yellow Pages. The latter is found in many larger cities. It lists those businesses whose customers are primarily or exclusively businesspeople. Thus, while you may find lists of local general-interest magazine publishers in a standard Yellow Pages, you probably will need the business-to-business Yellow Pages to locate the publishers of trade journals within your area. In my area, public relations firms only advertise in the business-to-business directory, while in some California cities, I find about half the agencies are exclusively in one book or the other.

By looking through the Yellow Pages you may also find potential markets for your writing. Companies may need annual reports, corporate histories, and similar writing on a freelance basis. If you see a company that seems interesting to you, call to see how their advertising and/or PR are handled. If there is no agency or department, talk with the president or his/her secretary for a referral. Business of this type comes from a combination of luck and creativity, and can help supplement your income while developing contacts in the field where you want to be working.

Other items you will need, both to organize your writing area and to assure you maintain proper records, include the following: file folders, a filing system for telephone numbers and addresses (I prefer a Rolodex, though any loose-leaf system will work; you can also use a computer), audiocassette holders if you interview much with tape, and a computer disk holder if you use a computer. In addition, it helps to have some 9x12 and 10x13 envelopes and one or more accordion file holders for long-term storage. A filing cabinet, including the inexpensive variety (store heavy books on top to prevent the file from tipping over when you pull out the top drawer) will be helpful. Other items should include a notepad, telephone message pad, or the easy-stick type notes, and a bulletin board. Some novelists also like a chalkboard or giant pad of paper meant for use when illustrating talks at meetings so they can note characters, plot convolutions, and the like instead of having notes to this end scattered through several notebooks, written on scraps of paper, and generally stuck in piles. The late Jacqueline Susann, whose "steamy" best sellers were known for elaborate casts of characters, kept careful lists of characters and their interrelationships so there would be no problem with consistency throughout her books. You should also have some form of ledger book for recording money that comes in (hopefully) and money that is spent on writing (inevitably).

For the IRS, you do not need an elaborate system, though you will want enough order that you can always find receipts and similar tax time needs. The simplest is to take twelve file folders and mark one for each month. Then put all your receipts for deductible expenses into the appropriate folder as they come in. These will be receipts for restaurant meals with editors or interview subjects (mark the purpose of the meal on the receipt as well as the full date and the amount spent), typing paper, computer disks, and other purchases.

You should also have an appointment calendar on which you note various meetings. If your deductions are questioned, the notation of a lunch meeting with an editor or subject will help to corroborate the receipt's validity.

In addition, keep a bound entry book in which you record all income and expenses. Note checks received, as well as the source. Likewise note all expenses and the reasons for them. Make the entries continuous, adding the total for each month at the end of that month's entries. Do this even though you are keeping your file folders filled with receipts and checkbook stubs for money paid out.

Other items you may need close at hand will vary with the work you do. A cassette recorder may be necessary to play interview tapes or to record telephone calls. (Check with the attorney general's office in your state to learn whether or not you are required to tell the person on the other end of the line that you are recording. There is almost a 50-50 split between states with such requirements and states without them. Federal law does not require you to tell the other party.) You may even need a videotape recorder or video player and monitor. Whatever equipment you need should be placed for easy access just as you plan for reference books.

THE IRS

The IRS can be a friend (of sorts) or a major drain on your limited time, depending upon your records. Even if you are unpublished and may be months from your first sale, actively working at your writing as a business will allow you many of the same deductions as other small businesses. Because the tax laws are regularly changing, you will have to obtain specifics from an accountant or tax lawyer, but the following will be a help.

Keep a consistent location for your work as a writer and use it for nothing else. Ideally this will be a separate room or a work area you've created. For example, a former student of mine converted an unneeded closet into a micro-office. It may also be a definable corner of a room used for other purposes. Whatever the case, its sole purpose should be for your work.

Keep all receipts from the post office (for postage related to your writing only), office supply stores, and note your mileage whenever you drive to an interview. The latter includes an odometer reading of the mileage at the start and a second reading when you return.

Finally, remember that the IRS wants to take its fair share, not to harass the average writer. Unfortunately, a writer not only has the power to make a disproportionate income, he can also find himself with nothing but "outgo." For example, during my first year of freelancing full time, I was spending $100 a month on postage, long distance telephone calls, and writing supplies. Unfortunately I was averaging only $25 per month income from writing! Terrified that these disproportionate expenses could serve as a "red flag" for an auditor, I sent copies of the writing that I was trying to sell along with

my tax returns. I explained that this was the product I was trying to sell that no one was buying. I didn't know if the IRS people liked or disliked my work, but at least I could prove I was
trying.

KEEPING CURRENT

No matter whether you have one or more projects un-
derway at one time, no matter whether you are writing fiction
or nonfiction, you are going to have to find a way to keep track
of each activity. Sometimes this is fairly simple. For example, I
am writing a series of novels that take place in Cleveland. I
have a file folder that includes maps, photographs of the city,
restaurant reviews and prices, and other information. I do
this with every city I use as background for fiction, regardless
of where I may be living at the time. Even if it is possible to get
in my car and go to one of these places, inevitably I need to de-
scribe it accurately at an hour when either the location is
closed or I am too tired to want to bother driving around
town.

Writers of historic fiction often go to greater lengths.
They will have picture files of clothing, weapons, transportation, terrain, and anything else that relates to the time and setting. Stuart Kaminsky has a series of Toby Peters novels that
take place during the 1940s. His books are filled with product
names, prices, and other details gleaned from newspapers,
magazines, and other period sources. The references come
naturally in his stories, yet give the books a sense of authentici-
ty that makes them popular. Less careful organization and attention to detail would make the books less interesting to his
readers.

It is important to keep materials for current projects
close at hand, including any records you must keep. Art writer
Sherry Brown simply has a folder for each artist, the files in a
drawer near her desk. By contrast, Kitty Kelley, the writer of
unauthorized biographies on Frank Sinatra, Jackie Onassis,
and others, keeps such careful notes that every telephone call

and telephone call attempt is logged. She regularly faces the threat of lawsuits and must be able to document everything that she writes.

What type of work are you doing? If you are writing articles, you will need one or more notebooks for interviews, file folders to hold clippings, reference material, photocopies, etc. If you tape record, you will also want a filebox or other holder to keep cassettes in one place. A book-type organizer that can hold a dozen cassettes is ideal

Nonfiction books are not much different from articles, though the volume of material you will accumulate is often substantially greater.

Fiction is usually the easiest to organize. One or more file folders for reference materials will often suffice.

Have a way to store your materials. A file cabinet is ideal for any quantity. You can also buy special organizers that fit on your desk and are slotted to hold file folders as well as other supplies. Your volume of work will determine what is most appropriate for you to use.

Next, keep a calendar that shows the deadlines for your various projects. Mark it in any way that will remind you to mail the work on time. For example, if your deadline is July 23, you might make a notation on July 14 so that you still have time for last-minute calling and/or polishing. Writers who produce seasonal material sometimes maintain two calendars, one six months ahead of the other. This helps them get in the proper mood for writing about Christmas in July or Easter in November.

No matter how you keep track, be certain the schedule you set is right for you. Your life and work are unique. Depending upon your circumstances, you may need more or less times than someone else.

CURRENT PROJECT PLANNING CHECKLIST

1. How much writing can you average per week? Imagine the worst possible month, with everything going wrong, and

determine how many pages you can realistically complete in that period. Use this figure when determining what deadlines you can always meet. In fact, there will be weeks when your output is much greater. But commit according to the worst-case scenario.

2. It is a rule that the closer you get to deadline, the fewer people you will be able to reach for interviews. Call and make interview arrangements the moment you have an assignment. If you are working on speculation, do all the interviews in as short a period of time as you can. When you begin writing you do not want the interruption of trying to run down a source. Murphy's Law for writers states that the availability of interview sources is directly related to the time you have to work.

3. Complete all research before you start to write. Otherwise you will waste time making telephone calls or hurrying to the library. You may also find that a complete rewrite is in order because you missed an important fact that must be included early in the article or book.

4. When working on several projects at once, be certain the deadlines are realistically staggered. Otherwise you will become pressured, less effective, and the finished products will no doubt show it.

5. Make a list of all your projects and their due dates. Set your research and writing priorities based on the shortest deadlines you are facing.

PAST PROJECTS WAITING FOR SALES

Include in your time planning any past project that is saleable but unsold, perhaps collecting a rejection or two along the way.

There is no such thing as failure in writing. Every rejection, every unpublished piece, teaches you more about yourself and your work. As screenwriter Joe Dziglo says, "Every no is a downpayment on a yes." Much can be learned from work that has remained unsold and/or ideas that have yet to be developed.

Unsold work remains unsold for one of three reasons: It was marketed to the wrong companies or during the wrong season, it was poorly written, or the idea was not strong enough to be considered. An article or short story sent to the wrong companies or during the wrong season may be saleable as is. Typing a fresh draft and applying marketing information you have gained from your first efforts may be all that is necessary to make a sale.

Poorly written work may just need a fresh draft, again using skills you have gained over time, to become saleable. Since the writing was poor, there is a chance that there were other problems as well, so check your quotes and make certain the research was both thorough and proper.

An unsaleable idea will not be strengthened with time. That material should be discarded.

You may find a story or two in your files that, on review, did not seem to go anywhere. The idea was great, the story line strong, but something was missing. You don't want to discard the project, but you also don't want to continue spending time on what appears to be a lost cause. Such material should be filed until later when time and distance may give you the perspective to effectively rewrite it.

The easiest way to handle the organizing of past projects is to use a system of file folders marked with the name of the month. You place your work in the files, then check them during the first week of each month.

Suppose you have trouble with a short story in July. Place the manuscript in the September file. That will give you two months of distance and other writing experience before you look at it again. The same is true with other types of writing.

Seasonal material will also go into the file folders. Pick the month appropriate for the lead time, generally six months. You will have three months' lead time for most monthly magazines so starting to sell six months early gives you time to have a rejection or two should you send the material to a market that doesn't respond with an acceptance and a check.

Each month you must review the file folder for that month. Some of the work should be read with an eye towards marketing it again. Other work should be read with the thought of rewriting. Any work that you feel is worth saving for review but which you are not ready to handle should be moved forward a month or two. In that way, you will remain on top of all projects that still have potential for sales.

Such reviews may help in one other way, too. You may see a new approach or a way to adapt the information you set aside for a totally different project. In effect, you are rejecting the old and discovering a fresh approach you previously overlooked.

CLIPS AND IDEAS

The idea file is a special file designed to help you with future material. As you read newspapers and magazines, as you talk with others, even as you interview for assignments, you come across ideas that will make potentially strong articles or the basis for fiction. A local article may have a regional or national twist. A national article may have a regional or local slant. Or your interview may reveal some interesting people or facts you feel could be followed up for future writing. Whatever the case, when you encounter leads like these, place them in a file folder.

You can be as elaborate as you want. You might have one folder for all clippings, as I do. Or you might divide the clips and the notes by seasonal material, juvenile and young adult markets, trade journals, and any other categories appropriate for the types of writing you are doing. Whatever the case, this file should be kept separately and reviewed whenever you have difficulty coming up with ideas. (Note: Some writers place clips and ideas about seasonal material in their monthly files for six months before the specific season. That way they are "seasonally inspired" during the appropriate time.)

PLANNING SALES

If you are typical of most new writers, you probably are freelancing at the same time that you are holding a full-time job. How much you can do with a full-time job will vary with your hours. If you work evenings or graveyard shifts, you will be more flexible than if you work days. Generally, most people find that when they work days with inflexible hours, it is not realistic to seek local public relations or advertising work. The work can be completed around their schedules, but often they can't get the time off needed to make the contacts those fields require. Should you have time off coming to you, sick days or personal leave days you can take, or a situation where you can trade time with someone on another shift, then seeking PR and advertising appointments might be feasible.

By contrast, local and regional magazines can be solid markets no matter what your normal work schedule. These include city magazines, state magazines, regional business publications, weekly newspapers, Sunday magazines within your daily paper, and the like. Your queries can be handled by mail. Your interviews can be arranged to your convenience in most instances. And the income will gradually free you to work only part time or to freelance entirely.

National work can be handled in the same manner as regional magazines. The mail works on your behalf, and a long distance service for your home that has a calling card or computer access system (such as Sprint, MCI, AT&T, etc.) will enable you to do interviews from any telephone, charging it to your home phone.

One additional time-saver is to always query when you are busiest. This may sound ridiculous, but getting an assignment or a speculative go-ahead from a query letter will take from four to eight weeks and sometimes longer. If you wait until all your writing is completed before seeking new work, you will have gaps in your earnings that will reduce the chance for being able to write full time. At first, try doing queries every two weeks or more frequently, depending upon your rate of success. When your sales increase, start querying approxi-

mately three months before you know you will be finished
with current projects. That should give you adequate lead
time to always have assignments coming in without having
new and current work overlap to such a degree that you cannot meet the deadlines.

CORRESPONDENCE

Correspondence should be divided into three categories,
either in folders or in a sectioned desk divider. The first are
the letters you need to write. While some writers include
queries in this category, I look upon them as something totally
separate. Letters to write may involve obtaining information,
thanking people for their help, personal correspondence,
and the like.

The second section involves letters to file. These include
copies of correspondence you've sent, letters from editors giving assignment or accepting work, and personal correspondence that you wish to save. Before going into this pile, the assignment letters should first be filed with the monthly "to do"
records so you don't overlook an assignment that has come in.
You will also find that by having the letter available, you will
not forget any of the instructions the editor has provided that
may deviate from your original idea.

Letters accepting work should also be filed in the monthly "to do" files in one of two ways. If the work is accepted with
payment to be "immediate," file your acknowledgment in a
folder two months past the date received. Payment on acceptance frequently means within the next 45 days. Pulling the record for follow-up after 60 days is wise, though hopefully not
necessary.

If the work will be paid on publication, find out when
publication is expected. (Most magazines can give you an approximate time.) Then file the letter for the month immediately following the one in which the article or story is to appear. Payment on publication should mean within 30 days of
the date the issue comes out. You will not want to wait any

longer than that to check on your money if it has not yet been sent.

SUBMISSION LOG

The final tool to help you with your writing is a submission log. This can be as elaborate or as simple as you desire. Some people use desk calendars. Others use ledger books available from commercial stationers. Whatever the case, you will want to have the following information for each article, story, and/or book:

1. The title and a brief description where necessary.
2. The date sent and to which publisher.
3. The date accepted or returned. If the latter, make a note of the editor who rejected it. Sometimes an article is rejected because the editor personally dislikes it but the material is right for the publication. When that editor changes jobs and a new editor comes on board, you may be able to resubmit it without mentioning the previous rejection and make a sale.
4. The date payment is received.
5. If all fails but you are convinced of the sales value of the material, the monthly file (at least two months ahead) in which you've placed the manuscript for later review.
6. The date and issue in which the accepted material appears.

The log is simply a way of keeping track of your work. Most writers eventually find that they query so many locations, sometimes two or three letters going to the same publication at different times and concerning different stories, that they forget what is where. I know that more than once, before preparing a log, I had the embarrassing situation of an editor writing and saying, "We are interested in seeing your article. Please let us know when it will arrive and the approximate number of words," only to discover I could not remember what query was involved.

Although these approaches may take a little more of your time at first than you would like, over the years these preparations and habits will serve you well. You will find that with the organization of time, family, and materials, your writing time will grow steadily and you will work far more effectively.

Three

SETTING PRIORITIES

Whether you are currently selling your writing or just beginning your career, you must consider priorities with your work. There are several ways you can do this, the method you select being determined by your personal attitude and needs.

For example, if you are not yet selling, you should decide what type of work you most want to do and how you wish to enter the field. Barbara Geisert is a writer who has worked in corporate public relations but now seeks to freelance. She needs her writing to supplement her income if she is to work into full-time freelancing. However, she wants to write mystery stories and films, a type of work that will take longer to complete before she can make sales than if she wrote articles.

Barbara set her priorities based on the fact that she does not need money immediately so long as she continues working in other fields, and on the reality that her first love is fiction. She decided to start her freelancing with fiction, working into articles as well when she needed a more immediate source of income. She also contacted a public relations agency in need of freelancers so she could obtain periodic local assignments for nonfiction.

Once you start selling, priorities have to be based around contracted material. Whether you write for a book publisher or magazine editor, you will have to meet deadlines. Sometimes meeting deadlines makes the difference between being published and being rejected. This is especially true when your article or story has been slotted for a particular issue and will become outdated immediately afterwards. For example, several years ago a financial magazine called me when it was announced that gold ownership, illegal in most forms since the 1930s, would be made legal again as of January 1 of the coming year. The editor told me that he would like to run an article in the December issue on the implications and the variety of gold (coins, collector's items, bullion, etc.) available. This meant that, to meet the deadline, I would have to complete the article in twenty-four hours, then send it by overnight mail. It was a last-minute decision before the magazine had to go to press. Another article was going to be pulled if I could do it, but there would be no interest in the piece if it arrived even twenty-four hours late. As an incentive, I was offered double the usual fee, an arrangement that resulted in my working around the clock. I met the deadline and had a nicer Christmas with the money.

Other deadlines are slightly more flexible. A novel or investigative nonfiction book may have a deadline that can be extended if needed and if the publisher is notified of a problem well in advance. However, a deadline must still be considered sacred.

What does this mean? Set your priorities based on what

you would like to write and what you are contracted to write. Earlier I mentioned the formula you should use for determining how many pages you can write per day, with everything going wrong. Determine the work under contract, the approximate length of the material you will have to complete, and the number of pages you can do each day on the average. Then add your estimated interview and research times, including transportation. This will tell you how much writing time you will have during the course of the deadline period when you will be able to work on what may be more personal work.

For example, my work day is approximately ten hours, five days a week. Saturday afternoons are devoted to being a human being, spending time with my wife and getting away from the work. But Saturday mornings are for murder. That's when I work on the novels I have not yet completed. Only a novel rewrite is ever on deadline for me, so this work does not receive priority.

Fred Rosen, who regularly produces books and magazine articles under deadline, uses a different approach. He is trying to break into the fiction market but likes to spend several days at a time working on that type of work. His compromise is to work as long as six days a week on his nonfiction for three weeks of every month. Then he rewards himself by spending the fourth week on fiction.

You must decide what is most appropriate for you. Above all, though, contracted material under deadline must be your highest priority.

WHAT MUST YOU EARN?

To understand how you must plan to build your career, you should first look at your financial realities. Answer the following questions.

1. What is the cost of your housing per month? Include rent, mortgage, and/or maintenance fees as appropriate. Also include your average utility bill. (Total your gas,

electric, and water bills for the past year and divide them by twelve to find this sum.)

2. What is your average monthly food bill?
3. What is your average monthly bill for your car, including maintenance and fuel?
4. What is your average telephone bill?
5. What other regular expenses do you have, including credit and charge payments, insurance premiums, etc.?
6. What is your average monthly expenditure for clothing? (Again, figure your annual cost and divide by twelve.)

Now, total all these numbers and add any other expenses you routinely incur, such as newspaper and magazine subscriptions, club dues, lottery tickets, etc. This figure is the minimum amount of money you need to take home, after taxes, for basic survival.

Next determine how much money you are averaging per month from your current writing, even if it's zero. If you have made only one or two sales, put down nothing. If most of your sales are relatively small but you recently sold "a big one," ignore the higher than normal check since it is not predictable.

Now compare the two figures. Assuming the difference is great, you will want to do two things. One is to retain any job that will pay the bills or make sure that a working spouse is comfortable meeting family expenses while you try to freelance. The other is to look at how quickly you want to move into full-time freelancing and compare that desire with the type of work you want to produce.

If you want to write poetry or fiction, know that predictably it may be years before you will have the luxury of full-time writing. However, if your interest is nonfiction or if, like me, you like to juggle the two, then the following should help.

The best use of your time will come in getting regional freelance assignments on which you can rely, This may mean part-time work for a newspaper, magazine, or public relations firm (assuming you do not want a full-time writing job). This may mean freelancing an employee newsletter or other project for a large corporation in your area. And it may mean working for trade journals and smaller magazines that have trouble obtaining skilled freelancers. Whatever the case, these types of jobs should begin to pay bills faster than is predictable with fiction and poetry. You may also find that you receive enough assignments so that these small checks meet your expenses and allow you the freedom to explore other areas of writing that interest you.

SETTING PRIORITIES BY PAY AND PRESTIGE

Some writers feel that priorities for contracted pieces should be based on the pay they will receive and the prestige of the publication. The more a magazine pays, the more important the periodical, the higher the priority for that deadline. I disagree.

My feeling is that all publications should be respected equally when it comes to planning for the completion of contracted work. If you agree to write for a particular market, you must plan on doing your best. You must write as effectively as you can, constantly keeping the reader in mind. You must meet your deadlines in order, not being concerned that one piece will pay $1,000 and another only $50.

The reasons for my attitude are several. First, you are a professional. Any time you lower your quality or delivery standards for any reason, all your work may slip. You could hurt your potential by not doing your best each time.

Second, there is no way to anticipate the long-term importance of a periodical. A magazine that paid me a half a cent a word when I started out proved to have the audience I needed to reach for my first book. The book publisher recognized my byline from the magazine and knew I was knowledgeable in the field, so he took a chance on a previously unpublished author. And the periodical promoted my book. That led to sales beyond my greatest anticipation and an eventual second edition of the book (the latter selling five times the number of copies as the first). Yet I never earned more from the magazine itself than enough to take my wife to McDonald's.

Third, so long as you do not have overlapping deadlines, you should be able to work in order of due date regardless of what the magazines are paying. You will put a low-paying magazine ahead of a high-paying one at times, just as you will be doing the reverse at other times. Work according to their editorial needs, ignoring the relative difference in pay scales, and you should have no problems at all.

COMPLETION TIMES

Earlier in this chapter I mentioned interview and research time. This is an area you need to understand before committing to a deadline.

There are two main types of research. One involves talking with people who are experts in a field, witnesses to an event, or otherwise of importance to the story you are relating. The second involves going through written material which may mean books, public documents, or even court transcripts. In addition, you may have audiotapes to review or other work requiring your attention. The following guidelines should help you plan.

INTERVIEW TAPES

If you tape record interviews, or if someone supplies you with tape, you have two ways to proceed. One is to listen to the material, making notes as you go, then moving back and forth through the tape as you search for quotes and facts you need in detail. This is time-consuming and extremely foolish. A ninety-minute tape reviewed in this manner could take you five or ten times as long to obtain everything you desire.

The better approach is to have the tape transcribed or to do it yourself if you cannot afford an outsider. Occasionally you're lucky enough to be able to hire a speed typist who is a good listener, able to concentrate so intensely that he or she will be able to work a little over one minute for every minute of tape. This means that a ninety-minute tape will take only

about ninety minutes to transcribe. However, under most circumstances you should plan on a 3-to-1 ratio—three hours of
transcribing time for every hour of tape.

INTERVIEW TIME

Article interviews usually last no less than thirty minutes
and no more than an hour unless you are asking a limited
number of questions from a fairly large number of people. In
addition, you must plan on travel time, including going from
your parked car, the bus, or other transportation, to the person's home or office. Depending upon the circumstances, this
may be as much as an hour in each direction or more. In addition, if you are the type of person who needs time to plan immediately in advance of leaving and/or needs to unwind after
the tension of asking questions, you will need an additional
fifteen to twenty minutes or more. When I was first starting
out, for example, I needed time to review my questions and to
go to the bathroom several times (nervous stomach) before
I left.

How much interview time you will need and how many
interviews you will have to do to complete the project will vary
with the subject. Someone who is knowledgeable, articulate,
and able to provide details and examples may require half the
interview time of someone else who either needs prodding or
blathers endlessly. Generally you will not spend more than
five or six hours interviewing for an article, though that does
not include the travel time to get to each subject's location. It
also does not include your preparation time before each interview.

MAGAZINE RESEARCH PRIORITIES

Define the most important people you need to interview,
or the types of information you need to get, then plan on ac-
complishing those goals first. The research or interviews may

be for matters that are the specifics of your article. Or you may be seeking an overview concerning your specific topic. Base your selection on those people without whom you'll not have adequate understanding to do further research.

Your next priority is the locating of case histories. These are usually the stories of people who have been involved with the subject at hand. For example, an article on the stock market might require, first, an interview with a financial expert who can give you overall information on the market and how it works. Then you would want to interview investors for anecdotal case histories, selecting perhaps one who is involved with mutual funds, another who picks and chooses conservative stocks, and another who is a high-risk speculator. The case histories illustrate points made in the article and humanize what might otherwise be a boring technical subject.

If there is time and space, you might wish to extend the article into a related but not critical area that would be of interest to your readers. For example, suppose you are writing an article for *Modern Bride* on buying your first home. The first concern would be getting information on housing purchases throughout the United States, including single-family homes, townhouses, condos, and co-ops, as well as financing options. Then you would find newlyweds who would serve as case histories. Finally, if there was time, you would explore future uses for real estate (as down payment for a bigger home, collateral for a loan, second mortgage for financing college for children, as rental income, etc.). The latter would not be an important part of the article and could easily be left out without the editor caring. It is just an extra step you may take if time and article length allow.

BOOK INTERVIEWS

There is no way to estimate the time necessary for book interviews until you are there. I interviewed Henry Hawksworth for thirty-five hours in order to write his autobiography, *The Five of Me*. On the other hand, an artist whose life I chronicled insisted upon talking about painting in general, the history of art, and other subjects unrelated to his own story. Approximately one-third of the interview time was wasted insofar as the results did not relate to the book we were doing together.

Writing a book leads to other concerns. Will you have to interview others? Will you have to cross-check material for accuracy and to avoid accusations of libel? Will you have to talk with large numbers of people, sometimes for a prolonged period of time, in order to be certain your facts are reliable?

The only advice I can provide for nonfiction book writers who will be doing interviews is to obtain the longest deadline you can get, then go to work immediately. Even a year goes by more quickly than you realize. After a while you will have a sense of the relative pressures that will be upon you. Unfortunately, when you first tackle this type of writing, each writer and subject are so different that only first-hand experience will enable you to anticipate the time you will need.

Certain periods of the year may prove slower than others. Some people routinely take off an extra day or two for religious holidays like Easter or Passover. Likewise, you might encounter extended weekends for Memorial Day and Labor Day. July and August are vacation months, and some business people take vacations between Thanksgiving and New Year's. If you have to conduct interviews during any of these times, you will have more difficulty being certain the people you wish to see are available than if you must interview during other periods of the year. Thus you may have to allow for people being on vacation when planning how quickly you can obtain the interviews needed for your deadlines.

That's why it's vital to make initial contact and determine an interviewee's availability as early as possible.

WORKING ON SPECULATION

Most professional writers either refuse to work on speculation or curse the idea. Yet the reality is that even professionals will complete both articles and novels on speculation fairly frequently.

The reason novels are handled on speculation is a simple one. Editors know that even the best of writers may start a novel with strong characters, fascinating incidents, yet have no sense of where their story will end. They are unable to develop a satisfactory conclusion, delaying the completion of the book or making it unpublishable. By insisting upon seeing a completed manuscript from all but the most well-established fiction writers, they are certain of the quality of the work.

Articles are requested on speculation for a different reason. Several years ago, after the 1976 Copyright Law went into effect, a number of publications became worried about their obligations when an assignment was given under contract. Corporate policy became one of not giving firm assignments even when the editor knew that there would be no problem with the finished product.

For example, at the time this occurred, *Modern Bride*'s editorial staff suddenly started asking for all work to be done on speculation. Top management, fortunately no longer in power, reasoned that if an article was requested on assignment, the publisher would be legally obligated to pay a "kill fee" if the article was not used. (A "kill fee" is a percentage of the agreed-upon price to be paid when an assigned article is not published.) Work sent on speculation would not require a "kill fee" and so all writers were asked to work that way. The editors assured the regulars that there would be no problems, that their work would be used as certainly as if they were on assignment, but management felt no assignments should be made. Under the circumstances regular contributors almost all worked on speculation.

The problem with working on speculation comes with some less than honorable editors. They give you the go-ahead to complete your article "on spec." Then they may give the go-ahead for a similar or the same idea from someone else. (All of us are stimulated by the same general media and experiences, so it's very common for magazines to receive several queries from different areas of the country for the identical article idea.) Finally they will wait for the material to arrive, pick the article they like best, and reject the others.

When should you work "on spec"? The best time is when you are an unknown factor to the editor of a good magazine who wants to give you a try. The editor may say something to the effect of "I don't know if you are quite right for us. We're interested in seeing what you can do and your idea sounds like you understand our needs. If you're willing to do this first one on speculation, I'll give you regular assignments if your work is acceptable." With that type of attitude, it is well worth the risk for your career advancement.

MARKET RESEARCH

Sometimes you have an idea that is not adequately developed. You have no idea whether it is saleable, though the general topic seems appropriate.

For example, Jerrold Ellner, M.D., a writer as well as a physician, had an idea for a book that would discuss not only AIDS but plagues throughout history and their effect on people. His agent talked with Prentice-Hall, which was interested, but suggested the book needed more of a focus. The topic of AIDS had already been well covered and the rest of the concept was too general. He was asked to research the market for something related to his original idea, then try to develop a book project that would be appropriate.

At other times, you may wonder whether your idea should be an article or a book. The topic is interesting, but is there a sustaining story line? What information is available? What will be involved?

Questions such as these will arise periodically with your nonfiction writing. You have a general idea for a story or book but you have no notion of how saleable it may be. You will want to set aside time to research the marketplace.

There are several steps to consider when planning the time you will spend exploring the issue. First, in the case of a book, you must determine what, if anything, is currently on the market on your subject. This is done most easily by checking three sources. One is your nearest large new bookstore. (Go to several when possible.) Another necessary step to determine the competition is to check the subject volume of *Books in Print*, a group of large reference books you will find at your library. This source lists all books currently in print, arranged by author, title, and subject. Finally, to learn about potential competition, check *Publishers Weekly*, the trade journal for the publishing industry. Your library will have recent copies, Book publishers advertise new books in *PW* on a regular basis, but two issues are special. In February and then again in August, one of the month's issues will look like a small town's telephone directory. That issue will contain most of the spring (usually in February) and fall (usually in August) lists of what's being published by the majority of publishing companies. By looking at the ads and skimming the lists of forthcoming books, you will be able to get a sense of what competition your book would be facing most immediately.

If your topic is controversial, you must allow time for checking allegations presented to you by the subject of the book. Or you may need to interview a large number of important people and have to contact them in advance to be certain that they will cooperate. Whatever the case, you will need to determine the focus of the book, rival works on the market, what additional research you may need to do, and so forth.

How should you plan your time? If you have other projects going and this is not of immediate interest, use whatever time you can spare from deadline material. You may have to switch your writing schedule a bit to fit the hours of a business or library where you need to research, but in general it should be handled slowly, as you can spare the time.

If an editor wants the material more quickly, then you may want to make it a higher priority. It will come after immediate deadlines have been met. However, because each case is unique and the time needed for research will vary with the specific project, it's impossible to come up with a specific formula. Just remember to be as thorough as possible so you only have to research once before getting the contract.

SPEEDING RESEARCH

The following are a few ways to obtain research material where others can be of assistance. Some are designed for obtaining documents. Others will save you the time of trying to track down an interview subject.

Public Libraries Libraries are more than repositories for books. Depending upon where you live and what facilities you can use (museum libraries, medical libraries, university libraries, etc.), you will find that they may have computer-assisted information resources, interlibrary loans, videocassettes, audiocassettes, laser disks, newspaper files, clipping files, picture files, and other resources. You may also find that the answers to single questions which might take you an hour or more to research can be researched by someone in the reference department as part of the library's normal service. Those reference questions might include helping you locate corporate headquarters for various companies whose personnel you might need to interview, locating often obscure publications throughout the world, and finding business, service, medical, psychiatric, and other associations whose headquarters can provide you with experts in their field for interviews.

First learn which libraries are convenient for you to use. Talk with the heads of those libraries normally not open to the public. Explain that you are a writer and wish to periodically utilize the facilities for research. In almost every case you will be allowed to use them.

Next, learn what resources are available within each library and how you can utilize them. See what types of questions the reference personnel will answer by telephone. Learn whether or not the staff will set aside books you need when requested by telephone to save you time when you stop by. Learn the full potential of interlibrary loans which may give you access to books in other libraries throughout the United States.

The Freedom of Information Act The sending of a letter using this act (check the library for directions on how to do it—you do *not* need a lawyer) will help you to obtain government agency files on a variety of people and public concerns.

Corporate and Service Industry PR Departments These are not "flacks" trying to hide the truth about their companies' dirty deeds. These individuals generally will provide you with access to even top personnel and as many records as possible. Over the years, I have found that they are surprisingly candid, even when they know that a factual article will put them in less than the best possible light.

Museum Libraries and Research Personnel These people not only help you in regard to their holdings, but will often supply the names of experts who can answer specific questions.

Law Enforcement Division Heads Law enforcement officers are extremely open and helpful providing a case is closed. However, there are times when a community relations officer will say far less than the investigators. If a community relations officer discourages you, call directly to the investigator in charge of the division (homicide, art theft, narcotics, safe and loft, etc.) with which you are concerned. Invariably, that person will help you or refer you to someone who will.

Four

SCHEDULING

The first rule of scheduling is knowing how to pace yourself according to your natural highs and lows throughout the day. One writer awakens filled with ideas, anxious to write, even if it is 5 o'clock in the morning. A second writer works best at midnight, continuing until the hour when most people are just beginning to respond to their alarm clocks. In addition, there are times during the day when you have natural low points, periods when you are sleepy and cannot think creatively. And finally, there are times when personal responsibilities, job requirements, and other factors will affect your ability to work.

The first question to ask yourself is, When are you most creative? For me, the early morning hours are best. I arise around 5:30, walk the dog and think about what I will be writing. Then I return to my computer and begin the work. While what I have written may need rewriting later, I find that this draft is extremely strong, flows easily, and often will be far superior to anything I can create later in the day. In addition, I am able to work quickly, often producing ten or more pages the first couple of hours, By contrast, if I start much later in the day, ten pages may be my total output even if I work well into the evening.

Fred Rosen is just the opposite. His best work often comes after midnight. Still other writers start late morning.

There is no right or wrong about when you work. The important thing is to discover when you are at your best. Ideally this will be time you target specifically for writing, not working another job, being involved with your family, or sleeping.

What if you can't write during this period? What if you must be on the job or meeting home responsibilities?

The answer is that you must learn to write whenever you have the time. However, if you are tired or not thinking clearly, you will want to first take a short break to refresh yourself. This may mean taking a brief nap or using a meditative exercise such as closing your eyes, relaxing your body, and spending a few moments inhaling deeply through your nose, then exhaling slowly through your mouth. It may mean taking a cup of coffee and reading a few pages of a book or the newspaper. It may mean going for a walk. Whatever helps you clear your head of the cares of the day, your tiredness, and similar distractions will be adequate.

Even full-time writers follow this approach. Religious writer Charles Ludwig, the author of almost fifty books, arises at 4:30 A.M. and works until approximately 11 when he breaks for lunch. Then he naps for an hour after lunch, refreshing himself for the period when he normally would not be working so effectively.

Each person is different, and the way to best use your time is to look at both your energy level and the demands upon your time. When are you at your most creative? Is it early in the morning? Midday? In the evening?

What are the demands on your time during this period? Are you commuting to work? Taking care of a small child? Relaxing with your spouse? Going to club meetings? List everything that interferes during those days when you wish to be writing.

Poet Judith Viorst, in an interview by newspaper writer Leslie Hanscom of *Newsday*, commented: "I've done all my writing around a schedule of nap times and car pools. I had to do it as the chance came. I was always writing down words and scraps of lines on stray pieces of paper. Once I had to go to the supermarket and retrieve a check, because I had written something on the back. When people talk of the poet's life, I think of ME going through trash baskets."

In that same interview Viorst compared herself with her husband, Washington-based political writer Milton Viorst: "My husband can turn out pages every day, but I think I've done well if I end up with 500 words. I give myself a month to write a poem. I'm always reworking lines. Once it took me a week to think of the word that I wanted."

Next, see where changes can be made. For example, if you are most creative in the early morning hours, can you set your alarm, arise early, and work before you have to do anything else? If there are family pressures, can your spouse assist during this period, perhaps getting the children dressed and fed or whatever has to be done? If you have to commute to work, can you use this time more effectively by taking a tape recorder for dictation while you drive or a pad of paper on which to work while you ride public transportation? In some areas such as New York, trains are standard for commuters and some commuters use battery-operated "laptop" portable computers while going to work.

Never curse commuting time. Simply find a way to let it work for you.

Are you most creative during a period when you are on your job? Is is possible to juggle your lunch and break schedule so you can get this time to yourself? Never do your work when you should be doing that of your employer, but you may find that you can vary your break, perhaps trading off with someone else when necessary, to gain a few minutes of personal time.

Driving home should be treated the same way as going to work if that is your creative time. If you are at home and responsible for cooking when you are at your best, there is no reason you can't prepare food earlier in the day, then warm it close to the dinner hour so you are not disturbed. You can also have another family member handle this chore when that approach is realistic.

Other commitments have to be weighed based on personal needs and relationships. Take time to talk with your spouse, go for walks or otherwise spend needed time together, then write while the other person watches television or listens to music. One romance writer told me that she used to feel it was necessary to her marriage to sit and read with her husband every evening even though this was her most creative period. She realized that the reality was that they were both absorbed in their books, each oblivious to the other. Writing during this period did not make them distant from each other. They were still physically close, only she was finally doing what she truly wanted to do. Her productivity increased by 30 percent.

Other writers have talked of the need to have intimate time with their spouses. One confessions magazine writer told me she resolved her problem by retiring with him almost immediately after dinner, then setting her alarm for midnight. She would arise and go into the other room to work while he slept. Then, three or four hours later, she would return to bed for another couple of hours of rest. She got all the sleep she needed but did it in two segments. Sometimes he got up with her, reading or watching television, and sometimes he arose when she returned to bed. It was a compromise that enabled her to work and kept him from feeling that he was less important than her writing.

Look at all the tasks you must complete each day. Which ones require creative energy? Which ones are busywork? Which ones can you do when you are tired?

For example, you may have meals to prepare, clothing

and dishes to wash, cleaning to do, maintenance of your yard, car, and other items, chauffeuring family members, and similar concerns. Some will be unchangeable, such as the time you have to be in the office, the time children must be in school, the time for such activities as sporting events, church or synagogue services, etc. Others, such as the cleaning, the cooking, and other essential busywork, can be varied.

Take a look at your list. Mark those tasks whose times cannot be varied. Then mark those where the hour or day in which you need to do them is not critical. Now think about when you are most creative. Can you free time during this period by shifting your priorities? If not, can you find time when you are either almost as fresh or can refresh yourself so that you will be effective?

In my case, I always reach a low point between 2 and 3 P.M. each day. No matter how much sleep I have had, no matter how I plan my meals, no matter how I schedule my activities, I am least creative and alert during this time period. Thus I try to do anything other than creative work at that time. Anything I can shift to that hour I will shift.

Likewise, I am most creative between 6 and 10 A.M. I try to delay making telephone calls, talking with others, or letting myself have any interruptions. When possible, I even delay a fast breakfast because I want to use that time for writing.

Consider your own life, then make your changes accordingly.

QUERYING/CORRESPONDENCE/ FOLLOW-THROUGH

Freelance writing is an endless round of seeking assignments, getting the work, completing the work, and seeking more assignments. Unfortunately these efforts do not fit nicely into a continuous pattern. The nature of your efforts is such that you must constantly overlap activities in order to assure yourself of a consistent income.

First is the seeking of ideas. If you are writing nonfiction, this usually means talking with people in fields of interest, reading newspapers as well as special interest and general interest magazines. If you are writing fiction, this means reading, perhaps visiting locations, thinking out plots, and so forth. Unfortunately the ideas do not come on demand, so you will be spending some portion of each day thinking about what you can be writing, exploring topics about which you need more information, and otherwise trying to develop new articles, stories, and/or books.

For example, suppose you have to do some shopping in a local mall. If you are a mystery writer, you might be thinking of ways to commit murder or stage a perfect robbery in the mall. If you are a romance writer, you might think of a love story that could be developed there. Science fiction writers might imagine an unnatural occurrence in such a facility as well as the way the public would react to it. A trade journal writer might seek business stories by studying window displays, traffic flows, observing special merchandising efforts, and so forth. A general interest writer might consider the mall's impact on the business community, unusual people who own shops, work in the stores, or spend time at the mall. Whatever your skills and interests, you can adapt every experience to your writing.

Jot down ideas and set aside regular periods for sending out article query letters and book proposals. (Short fiction has to be completely written before it is sold.) As mentioned earlier, when you are working steadily, sending queries approximately three months before your work will be finished is a good rule of thumb. When you are not yet selling, try setting aside one out of every five to ten writing days for sending queries. This is also a good period for handling other correspondence. You will be using no less than 10 percent and no more than 20 percent of your writing time. These percentages are high enough to eventually prove productive, low enough to prevent you from becoming frustrated about taking too much time away from creating new material.

Keep a submission log as you submit. It takes only seconds to go from addressing the envelopes accompanying your submission to making a note in the log.

Telephoning will primarily be a part of the research process. You should consider this a part of your writing time except when you are familiar enough with editors to call directly concerning assignments. When that's the case, those calls should be handled during the same period as your queries.

DETERMINING THE LEVEL OF RESEARCH

Research planning is only predictable after you have some experience in the field. Prior to that, it will be hard for you to determine exactly how much time you will have to spend. However, the following should serve as a guide in helping you to understand what research may be involved with different types of writing.

Fiction

Period fiction will require accuracy not only in depicting events taking place during that time period, such as the Civil War, the French Revolution, or whatever, but also the social customs. What did the people wear? What weapons, if any, should your characters carry? How did they live? How did they prepare their meals? What was their entertainment? At what ages did they begin courtship and marriage? What was the language like then? The latter is important if you are going to use slang terms since such words have meanings that change over time.

Your general reference librarian can show you which books circulate and which books must be used in the library. Plan one trip to work with noncirculating books, then take home as many circulating as you need.

Contemporary fiction will also require some checking. If you use real locations, you must have the streets correct, the stores accurately portrayed, and so forth. If you are going to show professionals at work—police, medical personnel, etc.—

you will need to learn how they operate and, in some instances, where they have authority. For example, some writers gain their knowledge of police procedure through watching television shows which are notoriously inaccurate. A call to either the Chief's office or the office of the community relations office will gain you an interview where you can learn whatever you need to know to write accurately about your characters. Determine what topics you will touch on, then plan on some interviews in person, others on the telephone. For a murder mystery you might wish to talk with a pharmacist by telephone, then personally meet with police officers and coroner's office investigators.

Keep in mind that part of the fun of reading a novel or short story is being transported into another time, another place. When that period, either contemporary or historical, is shown inaccurately, many readers will be upset and refuse to continue reading your work.

The research for fiction usually depends upon your local library. Most of the work for historical material can be handled by going through books. The time involved will be extensive and determined by the scope of your research, the availability of materials in one location, and the number of related interviews that might be important. Occasionally you will have to contact a historical society for additional material, though this usually requires either a telephone call or a letter. Contemporary work may require contacting a chamber of commerce for information about a community, obtaining city magazines, and/or visiting the locations.

How-to Articles

Unless you are an expert in the area about which you are writing, you still have to interview one or more people who are expert. Once you understand the subject, you will be able to communicate it effectively. Generally, since the area you need to cover is well defined, you are looking at a maximum interview time of two hours.

Biographical Articles

Interviewing a living subject for such an article will require your being flexible. If you are covering a narrowly defined segment of the person's life, such as an unusual trip or an exciting experience, then you will probably be able to finish the interview in two to three hours, or less. However, if you are doing a more general review, you will first have to know more about the individual by checking newspaper files, magazine articles, talking with corporate public relations personnel, and reading books and articles the person has written. Then you will have to spend what may be several sessions, depending upon how comfortable the person is at talking and providing anecdotes. Ten to twelve hours of research and interviews may be quite realistic for this broader form of interview.

Consumer and Investigative Articles

Articles that may affect someone's life or livelihood require more thorough research. If you are discussing a product, you must be certain you have checked all aspects, good and bad, with experts in the field before you pan it or endorse it by giving it a favorable review. Otherwise readers may attack your judgment, something that can cause an editor to reject similar work from you in the future. For example, if you are going to write about certain investment areas, you should interview both dealers in the area in question (e.g., stock brokers) and investment experts who do not sell what they are discussing. The dealer may have the most information but the independent consultant may be most objective about each investment area.

There are also times when you may be writing about something where a lawsuit could evolve. For example, I was once asked by a small town newspaper to check out a rumor that an unusually high incidence of childhood leukemia had been noted in one part of the community. If true, one of the possible causes was a local industry's polluting of the water system. If false, the newspaper would be guilty of causing undue alarm and might lose advertisers or face a lawsuit from one of the businesses. Checking out the story, which I eventually wrote as a freelance feature, required talking with the local health department, hospital personnel, area pediatricians, and cancer specialists. I also had to talk with state health department personnel who were conducting a study of the cancer problem despite denials from the local health department that such a study was taking place. I interviewed everyone who might be involved, and my story showed that there was either a cover-up taking place or that local health department officials were ignorant of a potential crisis being investigated by the state agency. Either way, the careers of several appointed officials were in jeopardy.

While the rumors, if published without these checks, would have proven to be accurate, there was no way I could know this without making the extra effort. There would have been an equal chance they were false, in which case my story, lacking full documentation, would have caused me to lose any lawsuit.

How long did the checks take? Approximately three days of telephoning people, interviewing in person, and reading reports. Almost all other features I had done for this same publication over a two-year period took no more than three hours to interview and/or research.

If your subject is complex, recognize that only experience will be able to guide you in estimating research time. Plan for as long a deadline as possible. On the other hand, for most other articles you can assume that from one to three hours will be spent conducting interviews and/or reading appropriate reference material.

DETERMINING THE AMOUNT OF RESEARCH

Follow two simple steps for determining how much research you will need to do. First, determine the scope of your article. Second, research until you understand what you need to know in order to effectively communicate the information to the reader. You don't have to become an expert on cancer to write an article on "The Ten Most Commonly Overlooked Early Warning Signs of Cancer." Likewise, you don't have to be a gourmet cook in order to write about the "Favorite Recipes of Local Master Chefs." Your job is to communicate information, not become skilled in its application.

The same is true with fiction. You do not have to know every last fact about an era to write historic fiction. You just have to be able to research those areas that will concern your characters and their lives. Likewise, you do not have to be conversant with a foreign country through first-hand experience to write an international novel. Author Sidney Sheldon believes in traveling to the areas about which he is writing when doing a novel that takes place outside the United States. Yet the information related to the locales mentioned in his book *Bloodline* could have been obtained by visiting a travel agency. I know because I gave myself an exercise to find out. I made notes of all the details unique to one of the novel's locales (the unusual wind currents near an airport landing area, for example), then visited a travel agency to see what tourist information they had. All Sheldon's details could have been obtained in the same way I got the information. Certainly visiting is better, but you will find that without a generous budget or past financial success, any way you can reduce costs without compromising accuracy is perfectly acceptable.

One other point: Research only until you can communicate the subject at hand. You only have to know what your characters know as they live that portion of their lives to be covered by your book. Researching beyond these parameters will prove a waste of your time.

SETTING UP INTERVIEWS

To save time, conduct interviews in the least complicated manner. Some people insist on a face-to-face interview no matter what you want to ask. Most people do not care and are comfortable working over the telephone. In fact, using the telephone allows you to become a national writer while staying at home. You call subjects wherever they are located, explain that it is long distance, and they are usually happy to give you an interview. Only once, when researching for an article I was writing for *Cosmopolitan*, did a subject refuse to grant me a telephone interview, insisting instead that I travel from my home, then in Tucson, Arizona, to Washington, D.C. I had no travel budget for the assignment and had to work around that one individual.

More common is the experience of writer Lynn Galvin. She was writing an article about the medals given to participants in Volksmarches, a group walking experience quite popular in Europe and some parts of the United States. She called the manufacturer of the medals, told him that she was writing the article for *Numismatic News*, and he called her back, talking for more than an hour at his own expense. He lived thousands of miles away from Lynn but was delighted with the potential publicity, something his company had never received before.

Another type of telephone interview is done because you need a quick answer to a question. To research a legal question, you may want to call county attorneys, law enforcement officials, and other experts throughout the United States. Medical breakthroughs may require telephoning a pharmaceutical manufacturer in one part of the country, a medical researcher in a second area, and a physician who has applied the breakthrough and is based in yet another location. With short questions, many people are happier to talk with you by telephone than in person because they do not feel that they need to limit their time involvement to when they can arrange a face-to-face meeting. They may choose to call you from home, a club, or some other location away from their office, working the interview to their convenience and often giving you more attention than if the matter had to be fit into existing office hours.

Plan on doing as much telephone interviewing as possible. This does two things for you. It lets you write articles about people of interest hundreds or thousands of miles away, and it saves travel time. A local interview may require an hour or more of total travel time. An interview out of state may be prohibitive based on cost and distance. Yet most articles do not require your physically meeting your subject. This is especially true when you are using the person's expertise for background information rather than making him or her the subject of the article.

Try to set the time for your long-distance calls when the rates are cheapest and the people available. A West coast writer needing to reach someone on the East coast has a three-hour time difference. A call placed between six A.M. and eight A.M. will gain you the lowest rates, even though, for the subjects you are calling, it is between nine and eleven A.M. By contrast, a call placed after five P.M. from the East coast to the West will reach the person in the early afternoon, though your rates will be substantially lower than during normal business hours. Juggling your time in this way means that you will also save yourself money.

DOING THE FIRST DRAFT

Most writers with whom I speak are too concerned about the first draft. They want to start the moment they have the idea, receive a request for a speculative work, or get the assignment. They know enough information to produce an effective query in most cases, and that seems adequate. After all, the first paragraph of a query letter has to grab the editor's interest in much the same manner as the first paragraph of the article has to grab the reader's interest. In many instances the opening of the query letter and the opening of the article are the same. Knowing this, many writers try to start the first draft even as they are researching the material they need, figuring that they will fill in whatever is needed as they go.

The reality is different. You will work faster and more effectively if you wait to start the first draft until you know everything you will need to know to write the article without stopping. The emphasis of your article will be correct according to all of the facts, not just some of them. Also, the work may be better because you find the best possible anecdote for your lead. When you start writing too soon, you usually use the best material you have, ignoring even better concepts for leads that you may uncover later as you complete your research.

You write to fit the story when you wait. You write to fit your preconceived notions when you start too soon.

What does this mean? Do your first draft as you complete the research. Instead of scheduling time for it, research, interview, and think about your reader. Evaluate the subject of the article, its scope, and the people who will be seeing it. Then think about this until the structure becomes apparent and start writing.

NOTE: For longer work, or for fiction you have interrupted, there is a way to quickly get back in the right thought process for writing. The night before you plan to work on the material, skim through your notes and/or what you have already written just before getting ready to go to sleep. Then, during the night, you will find that your subconscious mind actually seems to work on the material. In the morning, you will be more effective as a writer than if you do not follow this last-minute review strategy.

Should you have trouble getting back into the style of the writing because of your time away from it, go back a few pages and retype the old material. By the time you have retyped four or five pages, you will be back in the style again.

PERMISSIONS AND CHECKING

If you are going to quote from sources other than your personal interviews, there will be times when you must check with the sources involved and/or receive permission to use the material. There may also be times when you want to be certain your quotes are accurate. The time necessary for this effort will vary with the circumstances.

Some writers try to pull expert quotes from magazine articles and newspaper interviews instead of contacting the subjects themselves. The writers do not realize that any number of mistakes could have been made between the time the original manuscript was prepared and the time the material appeared in the periodical. These mistakes could cause the quotes to be inaccurate. Thus, as a general rule, you should always contact the subject and do your own interview. Only in that way will you know if the material is accurate.

Sometimes you will find your subject talking about a field that is foreign to your knowledge. You want to be certain that you provide accurate information to your reader so you need to check back with the subject, reading the specific area of concern. (Do not send the person the entire manuscript because he or she may choose to edit it. Instead, call to read the portion in question.) This may mean a technical piece on construction, medicine, the stock market, or some other area foreign to your background.

It is not a good idea to try and sell articles and books that have long quotes from previously published sources unless you are specifically selling an edited anthology. Permissioning can be a complicated, time-consuming business. You'll need to locate the rights holder (who may or may not be the author), explain how you want to use his or her material, and gain permission, in writing, to use it. Often, a fee will be required. If your project is a book, your publisher will help you arrange permissions after you have a contract. For articles or short fiction, if you really must use a substantial chunk of someone else's writing, begin with a phone call to the publisher of the work, to determine who holds the rights and to inquire what problems, if any, are likely to arise in gaining permission. Then follow up with a letter to the rights holder, detailing the source, the author, the passage involved, and how you intend using the material. Enclose a stamped return envelope for the reply. After a month or so, another phone call can help expedite things. Gaining permission to reprint others' work can take months or can fail entirely, so be prepared.

Checking with interview subjects on accuracy or wording

is much simpler. In general, it will take no longer than three weeks to reach a subject by phone to check a quote, though you usually can reach the person the same day that you are writing the article. The reason for planning on three weeks is in case the person is out of town. Most vacations are no more than two weeks with another week of playing "catch up" with work that was piling up undone.

Obviously these are processes that will take very little of your time overall but may nevertheless delay the completion of the work by several weeks while you wait to make proper contact.

ESTABLISHING REALISTIC DEADLINES

Establishing deadlines is actually something that will take experience to do effectively. Earlier you saw how to determine the average daily volume of work you will be able to produce, regardless of the problems in your life. However, this does not take into account research time and problems that may stop you when you have a short deadline.

For example, suppose you know that you can average one page of work per day over the course of a month. You accept an assignment that is due in a week, then come down with a bad case of flu. You are bedridden two days, can't think clearly the third, and are too tired to give a full effort the fourth and fifth. The reality is that you will have to call the publisher or editor, explain that you are ill, and ask for an extension. The fact that within that same month you will be averaging your thirty pages, despite the flu, does nothing for the reality that during the one particular week, you will not be productive.

In general, each type of writing has several stages to consider. Fiction has the least pressure because it is usually completed before being sold. With short fiction, you first develop the idea, then can write it beginning to end in the time that you have. Long fiction requires the idea, the character development, and the development of subplots. You may have a solid overview of what is going to happen firmly planted in your mind, then find that there are days when you spend all your time working out subplots you had not anticipated. Either way, it is fairly straightforward when it comes to planning time.

Nonfiction will require research, interviews, and similar preliminary work. You know your approximate writing time. Next determine how many people will have to be interviewed for an article, allowing three hours per person to cover travel time, repeat telephone calls, and similar problems. Allow at least eight hours for in-library or museum research, longer if the subject is complex. Often your work will take less time, but if you are like me, you will find yourself browsing through other books, wasting time. It is best to admit such a weakness and plan for it.

The more you begin to sell, the more frequently the unexpected will happen. You are on a deadline, then an editor needs a quick rewrite of a previously written piece. Or you might receive the galley proofs of your latest book and have to read and correct those within ten days. Or a new assignment might come up, one so exciting that you do not want to turn it down despite your workload.

The answer to this stiuation is to plan for the unexpected as it relates to your writing. The ideal is to give yourself one free week for every four to six weeks you are working once you are selling steadily. When the unexpected does not occur, use this time to get ahead on your deadlines and/or to tackle a project of personal interest that may or may not sell. Remember, as I said before, writing is a growth skill. The more you write, the better you become. That extra time might be useful for trying that novel or screenplay you've always wanted to do but are not certain is yet within your skill level. If it is, you will make the sale. If it is not, you are one step closer to success in that area. And if the unexpected occurs, you switch to the crisis you need to handle.

Five

WRITING SMARTER

SWITCHING PROJECTS TO STAY FRESH

There are many myths about professional writing, such as the one that states that there is no market for beginners. The reality is that all writers are mortal. The demand for newspaper humor will not end with the death of Art Buchwald, any more than interest in humor writing ceased with the death of Will Rogers. Writing styles may be unique, but the demand for work in every field outlasts the life span of the writers meeting those demands. The work of unknown writers will be in demand so long as it is competent, because from the work of the currently unknown comes tomorrow's acclaimed geniuses.

Likewise there is the myth that a "real writer" always completes one project before moving on to the next. The latter is often said by a well-meaning, though equally naive friend who is trying to encourage you to finish your novel, your nonfiction book, or your other work before tackling something new. What you should realize is that staying with one subject until completion may be ineffective time management.

Undoubtedly you have heard about that dread "disease" called writer's block. This affliction strikes when you least desire it, rendering you, the writer, incapable of working. You cannot think clearly. You cannot keep your mind on the story, article, or book on which you have been working, You fear that you are incompetent, that you will never write again. At the very least, you spend hours of precious time worrying about writing instead of being involved with the creative process.

The reality is that the cause of 99.9 percent of all writer's block is known. It is called boredom!

When you work exclusively on one project, there is a chance that you will become bored with it. Despite the advice of your friends who are not professional writers, the reality of life is that no one carries out only one activity throughout the course of a day. Doctors see several patients, usually with different problems. Lawyers see several clients. Even assembly line workers, doing the same job, at least have the chance to perform it on a large number of items. (Assembly line inefficiency from boredom, the production equivalent of writer's block, has led many companies to experiment with robotics or group assembly practices where each worker can do a variety of tasks.) But writers often believe the myth that they are not being professional unless they stay with one project through to completion before even thinking about the next.

The truth is that to maximize your efficiency, always

have two or more projects going on at the same time. When you are tired of one, losing your objectivity, switch to the other and almost immediately you will have a fresh outlook. Writer's block is broken and you move forward in an efficient manner.

BREAKING PROJECTS INTO STAGES

All projects have two or more stages to them. Short fiction and poetry, for instance, can be broken down into the "thinking" and "writing" stages. By breaking each work into stages, then seeing how your current work can be handled most effectively, you will more efficiently manage your time.

Generally there are a few categories into which all projects fall. Some projects will demand all of these categories. Others may require only two or three. Overall the categories include:

Library Research including the reviewing of microfilmed newspapers.

Telephone interviews, both extensive and one- or two-question calls to experts.

In-person interviews, including the subject of the article or book if biographical.

Obtaining documents from government agencies and other repositories. This may be done through the mail in some instances, including Freedom of Information requests (described earlier) or it may have to be done in person, such as working in the National Archives. Many repositories requiring in-person research have lists of professional researchers you can hire so you do not have to be present, should you have the budget to allow this.

First-hand research, such as visiting a community to walk the streets, check out establishments, take pictures, and generally get a sense of the location.

Thinking through the overview of the article, story, book, screenplay, stage play, etc.

Writing the opening.

Developing succeeding chapters.

Rewriting.

The entire project may be overwhelming, but not if considered as stages. For example, spending a day or more at the library or other resource facility is simple. Look upon this as a unique project that just happens to be a part of the longer work.

Next come interviews. See each interview as being unique. Then, as you complete each one, you always have a sense of accomplishment.

You get the idea. By breaking down a project into its components and looking upon each part as a task unto itself, the work begins to flow easily. You eliminate many of the stress factors that would otherwise affect you.

I have often said that it is impossible to write a book. No one can do it. Certainly not myself, though by the time you read this, my track record will include credits as author, coauthor, or ghost of more than sixty books.

So how do I do it? If it is nonfiction, I write an article because I can handle an article. The fact that it may detail a portion of someone's life (biography) a small portion of time (history), a step in a larger procedure (a how-to book) or something similar, all requiring other material to have a full understanding, does not bother me. I write my article (chapter), find that it leads into another article (chapter), which leads into yet another article until, eventually, I have said everything that needs to be said about the subject and I have written perhaps three hundred or more pages. I have completed the book.

Likewise, my novels are considered a series of interrelated vignettes or short stories. I write about certain things that are happening in the lives of the characters, then discover that they lead logically into other areas. By the time I have finished telling my short stories, I have a complete, cohesive novel that reads smoothly from beginning to end.

Another advantage to breaking each project into sections comes when you are feeling tired and pressured about time. It is easy to reach a point where you tell yourself that the article or book is so involved that you simply can't do it in the fifteen minutes you have available. Instead, you do nothing.

By contrast, when you have each project divided into sections, your attitude becomes one where you say, "I don't have enough time to write or do any research. I think I'll make the telephone calls necessary to set appointments for interviews. I should be able to do most of them in the ten minutes I have available." You become more productive and make better use of your time because of the psychological difference in your attitude.

Eventually it will help to give yourself deadlines for each of the sections. Not only will this speed your writing, it will help you better organize your time.

The simplest approach is to look at your writing schedule one week ahead. By the weekend, you should have a good idea how much time you may have during the following seven days. See when you will be able to go to the library, make telephone calls, and/or go on interviews. Note the days when you will be lucky to have any free time or your uncommitted moments will be at such odd hours that research or interviewing away from home will be impossible. Those are the times you will devote exclusively to either writing or reading the reference material you have been able to bring home. By scheduling your time in this manner, you will never be at a loss for something to do and you will always feel that you are making progress on your various projects.

MARKING OUT THE STEPS

Each time you have a new project, identify its various stages in order to best plan your time. The following chart will help you. Be certain to identify your reader first, according to the publication or perhaps the slant your editor has requested.

Articles

First determine the scope of the article. Is it someone's story? Then you will have to first know what makes that person important to your readers. This is something you may have identified before querying or it may be that the person is a leader in a particular field and you need to check his or her accomplishments. The latter may be as simple as looking at newspaper files in your library or having a public relations department give you a background sheet.

Next interview that person or those individuals who knew the person if he or she cannot be reached directly. This is done in person and/or by telephone. Then write the article.

Is the subject a how-to? Here you have just two stages. Go to the experts to learn "how-to" if you are not an expert yourself, then write it.

Is the subject a more general one? Start with the research and/or interviews that will give you a broad understanding of the topic. Follow up with interviews and/or research concerning any specific aspect about which you remain unclear. Then do research for anecdotes (sometimes provided during that first interview, if you're lucky) and write the article.

Novels

Develop in any order both complete characters for all the main people and the general outline for the book. This means the beginning, a high point from which all action will lead inexorably to the ending, and the ending. Then develop your opening. Finally, work just one chapter ahead, treating each one like a vignette or short story in the lives of the characters within the framework of the novel. So long as you are moving toward that ending, you will work faster and easier.

Nonfiction Books

It is often easiest to consider these a series of interrelated articles. However, break down the chapters first so that you know where your research must lead and do not forget details that must be included.

Short Stories and Poetry

Generally, as I mentioned earlier, this is a two-step process. The first stage is developing the idea. The second is the writing. With short stories, the length restrictions are such that you cannot develop character and story with equal vividness.

IS MY WORK EVER "GOOD ENOUGH"?

Perfection. Such an elusive goal. But a writer has to achieve it, correct?

Of course, you're not perfect yet so it is probably best to warm up a bit before writing. You can take a course, read a book about writing, or talk with friends about what you will do "someday," when you have more time.

And then, when you dare to write, you probably will have days and weeks when nothing will come. Writer's block strikes everyone, after all, and it gives you a wonderful excuse to go back to talking about the writing you will do when you have "lived" a little and thus have something to say.

Does all this sound familiar? Many writers waste more time avoiding writing by practicing such nonsense than they do actually writing.

Now before you become angry with what I have to say, I have my own time-wasters. For example, I once decided I couldn't write until all my tools were ready. Since a writer uses pencils and I didn't have any readily at hand, I had to walk to the store to buy some. They were #2 pencils (keep this in mind—you can't waste as much time when you use a mechanical pencil as when you use a wooden one), all unsharpened. Of course, when I returned home I had to find a pencil sharpener, then I had to even the points, and then I had to make room in my drawer for the extras. Finally, after killing more than an hour, I sat down to write—at the typewriter. I have *never* used a pencil for writing. I use pens for making notes (more legible and less likely to smear) and either a typewriter or computer for my writing. The pencil ploy was a waste of time.

There are other tricks, of course. You can overresearch a topic because others won't know if you are reading for information you need or reading just because it is interesting. Peabody, our dog, and I take a long walk in the morning (legitimate) while he uses up some excess energy and I think through my writing, including developing chapters. Then he is most comfortable going out three other times before bedtime. If I want to procrastinate more fully, Peabody suddenly "needs" more walks. The fact that he would rather sleep than be outside during those periods is irrelevant. I want to avoid writing and he is the perfect excuse.

The list goes on. What matters is not how many ways you can put off writing but what you can do about it.

First, ignore two other myths of writing. These are:

MYTH 1: You can't write until you have "lived," because a writer can only write what he or she knows.

MYTH 2: You must be "in the mood" to write or nothing of value will appear on the paper.

The reality is quite different. First off, I have written about mass murder, adult victims of child abuse, multimillionaires, heart surgery, and numerous other areas. If I had to have firsthand experience, I would be dead, in jail, in the hospital, or down in the Bahamas while nubile wenches cooled me with palm fronds and catered to my every whim, and/or some combination thereof. You, as a writer, should write about what you can learn. Of course you can use your own experiences and observations, but no writer can produce very much work if the prerequisite is to have lived the lives of the created characters. In fact, books such as the perennial best seller *Gone With the Wind*, all Stephen King's novels, and countless others could not exist if all writers had this attitude.

The idea of writing only when you are in the mood is also ridiculous. How often are you in the mood to face a blank piece of paper or an empty computer monitor, knowing that they will remain empty unless you create a world that has never before existed? Ring Lardner, Jr., commented that writing is easy because you just stare at the paper until little drops of blood appear on your forehead, and his comment is not far from the truth. I joke that I am "in the mood" to write perhaps four times a year. In reality, I sit down in front of the computer for some portion of each day, at least six days a week.

Writing is work. For me, it is the most pleasurable form of work, the delight of my existence. But it is still work and that means I do not go singing and dancing to the keyboard each morning, drawn as if by the Sirens' call of ancient mythology.

To avoid procrastination, or at least reduce it to a minimum, have a set place (or places) to work. When working a full-time job, include the location where you hide out during coffee breaks and/or lunch to get a few moments of writing or thinking, not just your desk at home. Establish set times each week to write (even if this means five minutes). Be constantly aware that when you are not writing, you are cheating yourself. Each time you think about that spot and those precious moments, you should feel guilty if you are not writing and driven to complete the work. The consistent reminder of a regular workplace is an excellent tool to fight procrastination.

Do not feel that if the work does not flow each day, you should avoid writing. There are good days and bad days, especially when you are first starting out. By the time you are able to work on several projects, you will find that there is always something you can do—rewrites, reading, developing a story idea, etc. If you are working a regular job, there may be days you know will routinely be exhausting, leaving you drained into the next day. These will be good periods to do any running around you need to do, such as taking books from the library or replenishing supplies. You might also be able to do rewrites or research reading. Only creative activities may have to be avoided because of fatigue.

Perfectionism is a quite different problem. Writing is a growth skill. The more you write, the better you become. No matter how successful a writer might be, anyone can look at that author's work and find ways to improve it.

Some jobs help you to overcome perfectionism. Writers

who have worked for newspapers before or after starting a freelance career may have an easier time. They know that the paper has to be on the streets on a certain day, at a specific time. They know that no matter how uncomfortable they may be with the quality of their copy, there is a moment when the concerns are academic. The work must be typeset.

Other writers work for years without revealing what they are doing. They fear it is never good enough and their jobs (or supportive spouses) give them the opportunity to write without having to test the marketplace. These are the people you meet at parties who are "working on a novel" and have been for years. They are also the ones who will never get published.

The answer to the problem of perfectionism must come from within. Writing is meant to be read. This book is about time management, yet some of you may be wasting your time reading it because your needless perfectionism is preventing you from ever letting anyone else see your work. You are being stopped from publishing before you try the marketplace.

The best advice I can provide is to do what I have had to learn to do. This is to try and make each book, article, script, or whatever, *the best of which you are capable today*. You should also try to make it better than the last work you completed. It does not matter what you are being paid. It does not matter how "important" the publication. Make each work better than the last and make each the best you can do today.

This is obviously a compromise. It is easy to tell yourself that if something is good today, maybe it can be better tomorrow. However, you must force yourself to remember that writing is a "product" business. You must have something to sell. You will constantly improve, yet if you do not test your work in the marketplace, you will never be a writer. It is the cliché situation of "biting the bullet" and mailing out the work on a regular basis rather than letting it stay in the files to be reworked next week, next month, or next year.

I will make one compromise with you. By now you are probably saying that you are not objective about your work immediately after you finish writing. You need some distance.

The answer (unless your deadline does not permit this luxury) is to put your completed work aside for no less than twenty-four hours and no more than one week from the day of completion. At that time, take it out, do any rewriting necessary, and mail it immediately. You will be looking at it with a fresh eye while establishing a mailing deadline to reduce the temptation to procrastinate.

Eventually you will find that, if you are not tired when finished, you can immediately and effectively rewrite. Again, this skill comes from practice, from learning to distance yourself mentally from the project so you are objective about what you are reading. It took me several years of selling, including working for a newspaper, before I was able to write, go for a walk, then sit down and effectively rewrite. Just make certain you do not allow yourself any more than a week's time between writing and rewriting.

Writer's block must not be used as an excuse to procrastinate. As mentioned earlier, 99.9 percent of all writer's block can be "cured" by working on two or more unrelated projects at the same time. Irving Wallace regularly tells interviewers that he is involved with five or six projects at any given time. The ability to shift from one project to another eliminates the exhaustion and frustration that otherwise hinder your production.

In case you are wondering, according to therapists who treat patients complaining of an inability to write, the tiny fraction of a percent of writers who are not helped by doing more work to alleviate boredom and tedium suffer from a very different problem: a fear of success or a fear of failure. This has nothing to do with writing. It is a psychological problem dating back to childhood that manifests itself in everything they try to do, regardless of the job. The solution involves learning what past experiences have affected the subconscious, bringing these experiences to the surface, understanding them, and moving forward. It is highly unlikely that you or anyone you know is having difficulty writing for this reason.

PLANNING YOUR DRAFTS

In the previous section I said that you should set aside work for one to seven days before rewriting. This is true with multiple drafts as you are developing a project, though there is a short-cut for this process.

Most writers have learned to produce more than one draft of an article or story. They think about the chapter or article, write it, give themselves time to think about it, then either rewrite it or start fresh from a different angle. This process is repeated until the work is done to their satisfaction.

Some writers have created fantasies surrounding their writing. The late Jacqueline Susann, a novelist who was highly skilled at publicizing her work on "The Tonight Show" and other talk programs, sometimes would talk about working on different colored paper. The first draft might be on green paper, the second on red, the third on blue, and so forth. She claimed she produced the same number of drafts—in the same colors—each time she wrote. Whether or not it was true, it was a gimmick that sounded good to the audience and created an image in the minds of the people who would be reading her work.

The truth is that everyone works differently. For instance, my first drafts are written in my head as I walk Peabody in the early morning hours.

You should get your story or article written as best you can, not worrying too much about polishing it as you go. This may be done in your mind as you think about what you are going to say, or in fits and starts on the printed page. Either way, it is your first draft.

Next, take a look at what you have written. Does it "grab" the reader's interest? Does it progress logically? Are the quotes in the right place (nonfiction)? Is the dialogue realistic (fiction)? Is the pace what you wanted? Does everything follow logically, be it the order of the article or the way in which the story is told?

Your second draft ideally corrects any weaknesses in character, structure, plot, anecdotes, etc. Then this work is set aside for the short period prior to your final polishing and mailing.

Some of you may find that two drafts are not enough. You will need a dozen or more rewrites in extreme cases, one or two additional rewrites for others. The actual number does not matter. Multiple drafts are designed to structure your work, correct obvious mistakes, eliminate inappropriate material. Then the work is polished, grammar corrected, spelling mistakes caught, slight additional restructuring or minor additions made where necessary. Finally it is mailed. You work at your own pace, always trying to keep the number of drafts to a minimum, letting the thought process before you write begin to develop the final structure.

SPEEDING MANUSCRIPT TURNAROUND

There are times when you are going to be rejected. I am going to be rejected. Your favorite living author is going to be rejected. Writing is so personal that even within the same publishing company, one editor may reject an idea that a second editor would have purchased. One of my newest books, (which shall remain nameless here to prevent backlash against me) was rejected by editors in the same publishing company where a different editor, neither knowing nor, in all probability, caring about the past rejections, just mailed me a contract with a healthy advance.

More years ago than I care to remember, I was in awe of television personality Steve Allen. He pioneered the late night talk show concept, wrote a Broadway play, composed music, wrote articles and books. He was famous, financially successful, and extraordinarily versatile. He also wrote an article for *Writer's Digest* detailing many of his article and book rejections. In fact, when I recently mentioned this to P.J. Dempsey, an editor at Prentice-Hall, she laughed and said, "I've rejected Steve Allen proposals." Knowing that fact, I was able to see rejections for what they are, a part of the business.

Because you will get rejected, even with highly saleable material, you should plan for rejection from the start. Instead of researching the one market that will be right for your work, see if you can find several markets that may be appropriate—competing publications interested in the same styles and types of writing. By doing this, should you be rejected, you are ready to send the work out again. You have a direction in which to go and will waste no time in putting your work back in the mail. If you have to research where to send material next while you're already depressed from the turndown, chances are that you will not bother. The material will be set aside for days or weeks on end, eliminating any chance for you to make money on the completed work.

NOTE: It is a good idea, of course, to glance at the article or story before turning it around again to see if there are any glaring problems you missed. I'm not talking here about minor tinkering. There will always be a word you could change here and there. Just see if there are major difficulties you overlooked so a fresh, corrected draft can be prepared before remailing. No major errors? Then send out the material and get on with your newer projects.

SIMULTANEOUS SUBMISSIONS AND MULTIPLE MARKETING

The best way to increase your production is to more fully utilize the work you are doing. This means taking advantage of both simultaneous submissions and multiple marketing, two dissimilar concepts that you should understand.

As mentioned earlier, there are two types of simultaneous submissions. The first concerns query letters, and there is no reason why you cannot send the identical query to competing magazines. Should one or more of those magazines not be interested, you have not wasted any time. Since most monthly magazine editors take an average of eight weeks to reply to a query, the difference between a simultaneous submission of identical queries and the sending of one query at a time may be a time savings of several months. Just be certain that each letter is freshly typed so that it appears to be an original. Do not tell the editor that other magazines are being queried about the same subject at the same time. Instead of influencing the decision favorably, such an action may result in an editor's rejecting your query for fear the material will already have been sold elsewhere before the editor has had time to make a decision.

Simultaneous submissions of finished material fall into a different area of concern. There was a time when writers routinely offered "first North American serial rights" to a magazine. This meant that the magazine was buying the right to be the first publication in the U.S. and Canada to print your story or article. Not specifying exactly which rights you were offering usually meant that the magazine was assumed to have bought *all rights* to the material: you could not resell it to another publication after it appeared without asking the magazine to revert all but first rights to you.

The copyright law, passed in 1976, is still in transition after all this time. However, my understanding and the information provided to writers through such organizations as the Author's Guild which helped lobby the law through Congress, is that there are some unusual changes. Under the law, the writer owns his or her work and a publication is able to use the material only once unless special permission is provided in writing by the author. Some magazines use a contract to buy all rights and others do not. In either case, specifying "First North American Serial Rights" on a manuscript now might actually force you to give up some rights. Leaving this information off your manuscript will allow you to sell the same manuscript to noncompeting magazines without having to wait for publication in any one specific magazine. Listing "First North American Serial Rights" will lock you into the publication buying it in the U.S. or Canada. You'd have to wait to resell the material until it appeared in the magazine which bought those first rights.

Whether or not you can legally sell identical work again and again under the new Copyright act, there are still ethical issues to consider. You must never sell the same article or short story to competing magazines because one or more of the editors is likely to blacklist you. Finding material they've bought duplicated elsewhere causes embarrassment for them, even though it is legal under the Copyright act. This is also why some magazines will have you sign a contract giving them control of the material in the same manner as they owned it before the change in the Copyright laws. Know what you're signing, and what rights you're giving up.

To understand the potential problem with simultaneous submission of finished work, look at the matter from the viewpoint of the editor. An article comes in unsolicited, is read, and appears perfect for the magazine. The editor will then perhaps get together with the art director and a person from the marketing department, at least, to analyze what they have. Is the article cover material? Will a photograph or a mention of the topic in a cover blurb help sell the magazine? Is the article going to be controversial in a manner that would be offensive to an advertiser if the advertisement appeared on the same pages (an article talking about sleeping pill addiction, for example, near an advertisement for over-the-counter sleep medication)? How does the article relate to special and seasonal issues? Should it be used in conjunction with other material? The questions to be decided are many.

Finally, after what may be several hours of work by from three or more people, everything is done. The editor, now extremely enthusiastic, picks up the telephone and calls you, saying, "Hi, this is Hildegarde Hammock of *Leisure Lifestyle for Seniors* magazine and I just wanted to tell you that the article you sent us was perfect. We're going to run it in our September issue."

Now imagine Hildegarde's reaction when you say, "Oh, Hildegarde, I'm so thrilled I don't know what to say. Just yesterday, your rival in the cut-throat magazine business, Oscar Overdone of *Swinging Seniors Outdoors,* accepted that same article. You see, I sent it to both of you, never dreaming you would both want it. Even though you can't use it, I'm thrilled that you called. Tell you what—the next article I write I'll send to you first, and that way you can both have my work."

Hildegarde will undoubtedly say how pleased she is, hang up, and quietly vow to blacklist you forever. She will look for your name. She will distrust you enough to not bother accepting anything of yours, not only at that magazine but at any magazine for which she'll ever work. You cost her time and money. You embarrassed her. You should not have made a simultaneous submission to competing magazines.

And this is the key. Some magazines stress that they welcome simultaneous submissions so long as they are alerted to that fact in your cover letter. Others will accept them so long as they are told and so long as you do not submit to a competing publication.

Each magazine is targeted for a particular type of reader. A few magazines, such as *Reader's Digest*, are aimed for almost everyone. Most specifically seek a particular individual or individuals sharing particular interests (coin collecting, skiing, knitting, cats, etc.).

The easiest way to understand a magazine is to check two areas: their article leads and their advertising. The first two or three paragraphs of an article often are anecdotal and will give you a clue to the magazine's audience. The people who are quoted will either have information relevant to the reader or will be in a similar situation.

For example, *Ladies' Home Journal, Woman's Day,* and *Family Circle* all have articles primarily for women who are married, have children, and are in the 30-to-45 age range. These women may or may not work outside the home, but they have higher than average family earnings and discretionary income. The magazines address their personal lives, their relationships, societal problems they encounter, and home interests. The products being sold in their ads all indicate these facts. The articles all indicate these facts. And the obvious conclusion is that each would be interested in the same type of material from you. As a result, making a simultaneous submission to them would be wrong.

By contrast, suppose you have written an article that details how a group of people from several churches of different denominations got together to fight drug use in schools. That

identical article could be sent as a simultaneous submission
(and you would tell the editors in your cover letter) to a magazine for Baptists, another for Catholics, another for Metho-
dists, and so forth. This is because they are not in competition
with one another. Readers of a magazine for one denomination are unlikely to read the same type of magazine sold to
members of a different denomination.

Sometimes you can also cross over generations. For example, an article on how to buy a first stereo system could theoretically be sold to a magazine such as *Woman's Day* as well as
to *Seventeen, Boy's Life,* and *Cosmopolitan.* In theory, none of
these magazines have crossover readership so such a sale
would be possible provided you alerted each publication that
you were doing this. One magazine is aimed towards teenaged
girls, a second is aimed towards teenaged boys, a third is marketed to primarily single women, and the fourth is of greatest
interest to married women with strong family concerns.

There is one precaution with simultaneous submissions.
You should have no problem determining which magazines
do not compete, but if you do have a question, follow the saf-
est rule: When in doubt, don't.

Save yourself time by sending identical queries to competing magazines. Save yourself time by sending identical articles and short stories to *noncompeting* publications along with
a statement to this effect as part of your cover letter. But do
not send identical material to competing magazines, even with
a cover letter explaining what you are doing and even though
it is now legal to do so.

Multiple marketing is different from multiple submissions. Instead of selling the same article, you sell different articles to noncompeting publications, the articles evolving
from the original research. For example, a few years ago I
read about a girl named Kathy Miller who had been so severe-
ly injured when struck by a car that she was not expected to
live. After ten months in a coma, she emerged seemingly as a
vegetable. Then her parents were told she would never walk
again and she certainly would have residual brain damage.
She ended up returning to school, competing effectively in

her studies and becoming a long-distance runner. The article I read, just a few short paragraphs on the sports pages, mentioned that 108 nations had honored her by declaring her the "Most Courageous Athlete" of that year.

When I interviewed Kathy and her parents, I realized that this story was a big one. There were several angles that could be emphasized and that is what I did. I told the story of Kathy's parents, Larry and Barbara Miller, for *Family Circle*. Then I told Kathy's story from her own viewpoint for *Seventeen*. This was followed by a story on the Miller family's interaction to help Kathy for *Success Magazine*, and a story on Kathy's spiritual growth for *Today's Christian Woman*. All of the stories were different and, though some of the quotes were the same, they were totally different articles. I did not rearrange paragraphs on my computer. I took my notes, considered the direction of each of the magazines, then wrote a completely fresh article for each. I went after multiple markets for the same basic material. I did not make a multiple submission of the identical article.

Essentially a multiple-marketing concept is developed by taking an article and deciding who will care about the various aspects of the subject matter. For example, I once taught at a university where one of my students earned her way through school as a $200-an-hour "hooker" working part time in Las Vegas. I learned about this long after her graduation when she was no longer in this line of work. She asked me to write about it and the story ran in an area weekly newspaper. Then a more elaborate story, from a regional slant, ran in a state magazine. And finally a third story was sold to a campus publication. Each was different and meant for a different audience, but the research was the same.

DETERMINING MULTIPLE MARKET POTENTIAL

The biggest question most writers face is how to decide which project is appropriate for a multiple market. This is actually simpler than it seems, though it requires being coldly objective about your work. You must not let yourself be influenced by the fact that you are in a small community, if that is your circumstance, or that the subjects are "nobodies," or that "everybody" knows about the subject. A good story is a good story no matter where you live. If a "nobody" is worth writing about for even a small publication, there may be an additional market. And if it is true that "everybody" knows about the subject, why are you writing it?

Let's start with the worst-case scenario, a person you think is a "nobody" in a small town. Suppose you are "stringing" for a small town newspaper and have a story about an area gas station owner who is the high scorer and tournament winner at an area bowling tournament. This is probably as dull a story as you can imagine, yet it will earn you a few dollars for sending the facts to the local newspaper. Is there a multiple market for this story? Perhaps.

First, find out what the tournament was all about. How big was it? What type of bowlers were in it? Was the man's score unusual? Did he have any unusual circumstances that make the feat more interesting—severe arthritis, an old war wound, a crippling accident where, by all medical logic, he should never have bowled again? Is he a member of a church or synagogue? (Note that I did not ask if he regularly attends.) Is he a member of a club or organization?

Next find out about his other hobbies and interests. Perhaps he likes to spend his evenings sitting in front of the television set drinking beer until he is too sleepy to think. Or perhaps he collects miniature soldiers, has toy trains, builds cabinetry, or almost anything else.

What type of service station does he run? Is it an independent or connected with a chain? Does he sell tires? If so, what kind?

Why all these questions? Because they relate to a variety of publications that might be interested in an additional story. You will have already obtained all the information you need during your interview. The only time you will need to spend afterwards is the writing time.

For example, if the man belongs to a particular religious group, there is a chance that that denomination has a publication. There are regional, state, and national publications for most religions. Many of these will pay for filler items concerning parishioners or general members who are doing something unusual. The fact that it does not relate directly to church activities (though in this case the church might have bowling leagues or local tournaments) may not matter.

The service station connection is important because of the variety of related trade journals. There are publications put out by various oil companies for the people who sell their products. Other trade magazines such as *Modern Tire Dealer* should be considered. You should always utilize the current *Writer's Market*, as well as asking the interview subject and others in the same business about the trade journals they receive. Each is a possible market.

Clubs and organizations are the same way. Many have local, regional, and/or national magazines. These will have varying pay scales, but your research was completed after you finished your interview. You can only benefit from the additional writing.

The hobbyist market is an excellent one. In addition, you may find a second story, one even more saleable than your original bowling assignment. This is especially true with the trade journals related to your subject's business.

All interviews should be explored the same way. When you write a local article, there may be regional or national slants you can use for resale. A national article may have a regional or local slant. And both types may have side markets ranging from trade journals to other specialized periodicals.

I have sometimes used this approach to find story ideas in articles other writers have done. I will read about someone in a newspaper or magazine, then look to see what other potential markets might exist. After that, a telephone call gains me all the additional information I need.

For example, I read about a photographer named Mick Palladin who photographed Hollywood celebrities, politicians, and others from his home in Carefree, Arizona. The people paid $1,500 per day to have him take their picture and were treated like royalty. He utilized a limousine pick-up with a chauffeur/bodyguard, luxury accommodations, and other services.

The article appeared in a state newspaper, yet that did not matter in terms of some of the markets. I called him, did an in-depth interview, then sold a cover story to *Studio Photographer* magazine and an inside feature to *Arizona Living*, a regional publication. Two or three other markets also became interested in him because he later challenged pugnacious actor Sean Penn to a fight. Obviously the writer of the original article could have done what I did and would have had a better chance to make the sales. Yet that writer did not think of multiple markets and I did. You should be doing the same.

Not every interview and every article will lend itself to multiple sales, but many will. In addition, see if the basic research, coupled with examples, can be used for a noncompeting but similar publication.

NOTE: Frequently, interview tapes you make when on assignment can be turned into radio features. Or you can redo interviews conducted in the past for radio, utilizing the studio's equipment. Most receptive are "talk" radio stations, stations that feature extensive news and/or magazine format shows, and public broadcasting stations. The latter are often associated with colleges and universities. In every case, contact either the program director or the general manager. Outside your immediate area, locate stations through the Broadcasting Magazine *annual yearbook. Your library should have a copy.*

There are numerous magazines related to personal and business financial matters for professions. These include *Physician's Management, Dental Management, Medical Economics, Veterinary Economics, Optometric Management*, and numerous others. An article on a business aspect affecting each professional field can be sold to all of them. The examples must change, of course, a veterinarian not wanting to read about an MD, and neither wanting to read about an optometrist. Yet all of them often face similar problems with malpractice issues, personal investments, staff relations, and the like. Each time you interview experts in one field, ask them about the other. Obtain case histories related to the different fields. Then write a fresh article for each different publication; your basic research is already done. This takes somewhat more time than the previous approach, but far less time than completely original research. More important, your ultimate pay will be several times that of your initial effort. Again, such guides as the current *Writer's Market* will lead you to the appropriate publications.

THE PROBLEM OF SUBRIGHTS

Books present different challenges for multiple marketing. Many books, especially those in the hobby and how-to fields, are naturals for spinoff articles. However, before you consider such ways to maximize your time, you must be aware of the field of subrights.

When a book publisher buys a book, the company is not counting on the book sale alone to make money, but looks at a variety of ways to exploit the product, each of which will bring money to the company. Your contract will call for a split of the cash, each of you benefiting.

What the publisher does not tell you is that you could just as easily make many of these sales yourself. Often a writer will sell some of what would otherwise be subrights before approaching a book publishing company. At other times, the writer will make such sales without realizing how the business works. Unfortunately the more of these rights that no longer exist at the time the book is sold, the lower the advance you will be offered.

The most common subrights sales include paperback rights, book club rights, movie rights, overseas book rights, magazine rights, and newspaper rights. Some of these cannot be sold without the book being accepted by the publisher. You cannot have a paperback subrights sale if there is not first a hardback sale. (A book sold as a "paperback original" will obviously only have the one-time sale.) Likewise, the book clubs are not going to go to you and give you money for the use of a book you have not sold. Thus, in the majority of instances, you can safely presume that a book will sell to paperback houses and book clubs only through the publisher.

Movie rights are another matter. It is quite possible to sell the rights to an unpublished novel or nonfiction book. In fact, it is done with some frequency by knowledgeable writers.

For example, my first movie sale, *The Five of Me*, was made through the publishing company. Because of the split with the publishing company and the subject of the book, I ended up receiving a total of $5,000 for the movie project. Recently, when faced with a book with excellent screen potential, I sold the rights to the unsold, unpublished book to the film industry. Though I again had to split the profits with another person, because of my approach, my total income will exceed ten times what I earned for my first book-to-movie deal.

This may seem like a wonderful idea, but you must look at what I did from the viewpoint of the publisher. The book involved is one that has excellent potential for sale. It should do well on its own. But suppose it doesn't? Suppose no one wants the book after the publisher has spent many thousands of dollars preparing and marketing it? Under such a circumstance, the share of the movie money the publisher would have received if the company had been involved with the film sale might have offset losses. In fact, it might have made the difference between a loss and a profit. That profit might have been slight, yet it would have been there.

By eliminating the publishing company's chance to share in what could be one of the subrights from the sale of the book, I made the book less desirable. Perhaps the publisher would have to offer less of an advance, do less promoting, and/or go with a smaller print run. Perhaps the book would have to be rejected altogether. There are many concerns, far more than the writer realizes.

Should you try to maximize the time and income from a book project by selling too much of the book as you go, you may find that you hurt the sale of the book. Or you may make the book sale but hurt the subrights.

EVALUATING YOUR NONFICTION BOOK

The following questions should be answered concerning a nonfiction book project. They will help you determine to what degree you can make additional money from the same research without hurting the subrights sales.

1. What is your book's subject classification? Is it (A) a biography; (B) history; (C) science; (D) art or architecture; (E) business; (F) hobby; (G) do-it-yourself; (H) other?

2. What is your predictable target audience? Is your material appropriate to other age groups? If so, make note of them.

3. What are the magazines read by people who might buy your book? Limit your selection to only those which relate to the subject of the book. A market guide such as *Writer's Market* will help. Be certain to check all listings, including trade journals and special interest publications.

4. What aspects of your research might interest the readers of the magazines listed in question 3? Think in terms of articles that could be developed from the research rather than trying to sell chapters in their final form. Chapters offered for sale will be part of what are known as "serial rights" when the book is completed. You do not want to interfere with such sales. Using the research for articles, on the other hand, is multiple marketing.

5. What aspects of your book will be newsworthy, either on a national level or within your field? Newspaper syndicates may be interested in articles based on this information. Again, however, these may best be saved for marketing directly with the book to increase sales.

6. Looking at your answers for questions 4 and 5, which of your answers for question 4 are *not* among your answers for question 5? These are the subject areas that will be best for multiple marketing before the book is sold.

With this information, you have actually put together a marketing guide to enable yourself to make the most efficient use of the time you have put into your book. Take the article areas you have discovered through answering these questions and prepare query letters. Your research will be completed so all you will have to do is write. You will be able to earn money as you go; you've used your time most efficiently.

In considering subrights and spinoff articles from your research, the best advice is simply this: Do not get into a position where what seems like good time management and a chance to make more money from your unsold book actually hurts eventual income.

When a publisher considers subrights promotions, the first concern will be any information, facts, or startling revelations that can be used to sell the book to a target market. A biography, history, or science book might contain something so newsworthy that it can make newspaper copy, magazine articles, and similar areas of interest. Celebrity books often fit into this category and lead to the excerpts you see in the *National Enquirer*, the *National Star, Cosmopolitan, Ladies' Home Journal,* and numerous other publications of all sizes and types. Sometimes these are also syndicated to daily newspapers both in the United States and abroad. These excerpts can run from 2,500 words to 10,000 words or more.

At other times the information is not of national importance but it should make a strong impact on a narrower audience. This can be a new discovery in the hobby field, a new business technique, or almost anything else, depending upon your book. The topic may make headlines only in trade journals and special interest periodicals, but it is just as important to those readers as national news might be to others.

These items of special interest are the ones the publisher will not want released before your book is on the market. They encourage publications to give you special publicity through articles that will appear at the same time the book is released. They help gain the greatest attention at the time it matters most—when your book is in the stores.

NOTE: Publishers have found that readers generally have a three-day retention period when they become interested in a book. If they cannot find the book in the stores within three days of hearing about it, they will buy something else. They usually will not remember it and keep looking, no matter how enthusiastic they may have been when they first learned about it. Thus, writing you do about your subject before the book appears is likely to be of no value in the marketing of your book. It may establish you as being a knowledgeable expert among those who read it, if they check the bylines and see your name with enough frequency. But it will not be likely to sell the book. Thus you should not think that releasing newsmaking stories early will help your sales. If anything, it will hurt them.

SPECIAL ADVICE FOR WRITERS OF SHORT MATERIAL

While I've covered most areas of concern regarding marketing, there are a few tricks you can use when you are writing short stories and poetry. Obviously you will generally not have spinoffs from original research here. However, you should look to two market areas you never considered.

The first is the trade journal. A trade journal is so concerned with business that most writers forget that the readers often would enjoy a change of pace *if and only if* it is directly related to their field. For example, several years ago I was teaching a continuing education course in professional writing. One of my students was a registered nurse who wrote poetry. The poetry frequently concerned humorous and rather sad experiences to which others in the medical professions could relate. She was trying to market it, but her efforts were aimed towards the traditional outlets, family magazines, magazines for new parents, and the like. She ignored the one area that seemed potentially most sensitive to her work, the journals for nurses and other health care professionals.

"But they never use poetry," she told me. "Why would they want mine?"

"They probably never use it because what they receive is not appropriate for their readers. Your work is perfect. Try it."

Not only did my student's work sell, one of the nursing magazines began regularly featuring a page of her poetry. It was effectively targeted for those readers.

Poetry, humor, even short fiction will often be publishable in trade journals if the business concerned is an integral part of the story or poem. A character carrying a camera and having an adventure would not be acceptable for a photography magazine if the business tool was secondary to the story. But if the story captured the reality of the commercial studio photographer, was fun to read, and truly showed that the writer had inside knowledge, the magazine might be likely to take a chance. Few writers consider this reality, so the submissions are almost nonexistent.

Newspapers are another overlooked medium. Both dailies and weeklies will experiment with good, short material. Periodically on my travels I will encounter smaller community papers that run a weekend novel. An area writer sells a novel (whose plot is approved in advance) that is serialized on a weekly basis. Some papers want stories only for children, to run on a "kids'" page. Others want them for adults. In both cases, the managing editor or the features editor, if they have one, is the person to contact. Have examples of the work and keep them short. This is especially true for poetry which will most likely be used as a feature unless it proves popular enough so that it can be turned into a column.

Newspapers allow an even greater freedom for effective time management. With a newspaper you can sell the same material over and over again so long as the publications are noncompeting. This means that if a community has two or more papers, including weeklies, only one within that community should receive your work. The *Editor & Publisher Yearbook*, released annually (usually around July), lists every newspaper in the United States by the city in which it is located. Your library probably has a copy. Study it to determine noncompeting periodicals.

Newspapers are generally interested in two types of features: "one-shots" and columns. The one-shot may be a seasonal article concerned with Christmas, Easter, or some other holiday. It may be a news feature, an in-depth look at something of broad interest that has not been covered by staff reporters or the wire services. It may even be an analysis of an event by an expert, either yourself or someone you've interviewed, where that expert's opinion is important to the understanding of the issue.

A column is a short (usually 500-750 word) article on a subject you will be covering regularly. It might relate to coin collecting, knitting, home maintenance, or anything else that has a predictable audience and a topic broad enough to continue providing material. The narrower the subject, the more difficult it is to keep selling.

Erma Bombeck has become quite successful writing a humor column that primarily relates to home and family. The topic is seemingly so limited, yet Bombeck's mind thinks in a way that continually develops new ideas, new insights, and new slants. She delights readers who have followed her work over the many years she has been producing.

By contrast, almost every person who has tried to imitate her by writing about home and family has failed over time. Their early work may have been excellent. They had a good sense of humor, strong writing skills, yet they found the subject too confining. Within a matter of months they ran out of new ideas, destined either to start repeating themselves or leave the business.

Other humorists, such as Art Buchwald, have not narrowed their focus. Instead, they have chosen broader themes, such as happenings in America or internationally. They may have a personal preference, such as Buchwald's interest in political satire, but they do not limit themselves to that area. Thus they can always find something that is stimulating and theoretically never run out of ideas.

Newspaper interest in freelance material will vary. Some papers delight in it, using it to supplement a limited staff. Others have little enough space as it is and do not purchase outside material except for that which they buy from a syndicate.

Advertising plays a major role in a newspaper's format. Newspapers add copy according to the pages they can produce when advertising allows. Papers have a larger "news hole" because advertisers pay for the extra space. News and features are fit around the ads, not the other way around. News and features will be cut from the paper or held up if the advertising dollars do not warrant the expense. Papers are businesses first, communicators second, a sad reality that a writer has to understand.

Newspaper pay for freelancers will vary with circulation. The greater the circulation, the greater the pay you will generally receive. One newspaper may pay $3 for a feature while a second has to pay $150 for the same one. Most syndicates feel that once a feature is in one hundred or more papers, the average gross income will be $10 per paper. You keep the full amount when you sell directly. You generally keep half the amount when the syndicate handles the sales.

Maximizing your time when selling to newspapers is fairly easy because the same material is going to noncompeting papers throughout the United States However, be certain that what you are writing has an appeal to more than one community. You will be offering a simultaneous submission and you want it to have as much appeal in Hilo, Hawaii, as it does in Bismarck, North Dakota, and Trenton, New Jersey.

Newspapers have specific lead times for their features. With few exceptions, newspapers rarely have shorter than a two-week lead time for freelance submissions of this type. A six-week lead time is not uncommon. In fact, in the case of columns, the papers want to see material come in at least six weeks in advance. This means that you must have at least six examples of a weekly column completed at the time you try to sell it.

Newspaper features can be treated like magazine projects where you query first to be certain there is an interest. However, once you have completed and sold a feature and you decide to maximize your time by reselling it to several papers, you will be sending the completed feature. You will not then query each paper individually beforehand.

A newspaper feature is seldom more than five pages (1,250 words), though it can go longer. Shorter work will appeal to more papers, though, and short, timeless features that a busy editor can use to "plug a hole" on a feature page have the best chance of selling.

NOTE: Newspaper features, as well as columns, should be sent to either the Managing Editor or the Features Editor. Material addressed to just "Editor" or to "City Editor" may very well be thrown away. The E&P Yearbook *can also provide the name of a specific editor to whom you can direct submissions.*

SIMULTANEOUS SUBMISSIONS

The following is a rapid review of the thought process you should use when making multiple submissions.

Newspapers

Poetry: Whether humorous or serious, keep it short and give it a direction. Poetry about business may appear daily or weekly on the business pages. Television commentary is for the entertainment section. Social comments are for the lifestyle pages (what were formerly called the "women's pages). And political comments are for the editorial pages. Do not offer a mix of topic areas because your audience is strongest when the reader can turn to one section, day after day or week after week, and always see your work.

Columns: Make them general enough so they can be sustained. The narrower the topic, the more difficult it is to generate new ideas. Five hundred words is the normal minimum; 750 words the maximum. Be sure your cover letter (ideally, computer generated for speed, the names and addresses the only changes to be made) includes your telephone number.

Features: These usually are 1,250 words maximum unless they're being serialized. They must offer something not otherwise available from a paper's staff members or wire service.

Mailing: Send all work to the Managing Editor or Features Editor. To save time, mail in batches. You might pick one newspaper in each city in your state or perhaps one paper per city, each city in a different state. It is cheaper to use a small self-addressed, stamped envelope (SASE) for the reply rather than an envelope and postage adequate for the return of the material. It is usually cheaper to pay for photocopies than to cover the postage and mailing envelope costs for the package. Remember to include at least six weeks' worth of samples.

Articles

Study the magazines to see who their audience might be. Think about the potential consumers for their ads as well as the sex, age, and family circumstances indicated by the tone of their articles if you are uncertain. Special interest magazines are obvious by their titles.

Submit your work to those magazines which could use it but which do not compete. Explain that you are simultaneously submitting to noncompeting publications, In the case of special interest publications, such as religious magazines and professional trade journals, there is less chance of a conflict so long as you do not choose two magazines aimed for the same religion, profession, etc. With professional journals, you may also need to change your lead and your examples to be most appropriate, though the rest of the article can remain the same.

Fiction

Generally, short fiction will follow either the articles approach or have to be sold in different countries. *Artist's & Writ-*

er's Yearbook, Ulrich's Guide to International Periodicals (see your library's reference section), and similar guides will help you to find appropriate markets. Thus, a short story might appear in a U.S. publication, another in Canada, one in England, France, etc.

Books

Study the nonfiction book chapters you are writing to see if there are article spinoffs from the original research. Do *not* try to sell individual chapters before the book is published because you may violate your contract and you will seriously hurt serial rights sales.

Novels generally offer no options for selling chapters. However, the characters or ideas generated during the writing for subplots, then discarded, might be effective for short stories.

BRANCHING OFF

As you can see from this chapter, there are many ways to increase your productivity within the time you have. The following is both a review of options and some new suggestions to increase your productivity. Look for the type of writing you are currently doing, then see the suggestions for branching off from there.

Articles: Simultaneous submissions where appropriate. Multiple marketing from the original research. Also consider developing a book on the subject, if warranted, or using it as the springboard for a book on the general topic. If the article is a dramatic story, consider selling it to Hollywood in the form of an idea (the article itself is fine for this), a screen treatment, or a film script. Likewise, a short story or novel might be a spinoff, using the article for your basic concept. Additional sales may be possible to newspapers through a syndicate (see listings in *Editor & Publisher*'s syndicate directory that appear within the magazine approximately every July and syndicate listings in the current *Writer's Market*).

Short Story: Simultaneous submissions are usually the best approach, ideally limiting your sale to one market in the U.S., then turning to an internationl listing for foreign magazines that might be interested. Also consider turning your story into a film script, a play (if the action can be limited to one or two sets), and developing the characters into a novel. As mentioned earlier, the Lawrence Block "Burglar" series had its origins in a character originally "starring" in a short story.

Nonfiction Book: Research for the chapters can be spun off into articles both for magazines and, where appropriate, newspapers (see the articles section here). When appropriate, consider a screenplay from the book. Occasionally the topic area will also lead to a possible novel at a later time.

Screenplays or Theatrical Plays: The logical spinoffs are short stories and novels.

Poetry: Newspaper sales, simultaneous submissions to noncompeting magazines, and international sales are the most likely outlets. Also consider collecting poetry on a consistent theme (*not* your views on life in general, unless you are a celebrity whose ideas people want to hear) for book publication. Some poets find that their observations on people or life in general, generated while searching for a poem to write, can be developed into short stories. The reality of this for you will depend upon what you write and your thought process in getting there. This is not practical for most poets but it's a possibility that should not be overlooked. Also consider the greeting card and related products market—calendars, wall hangings, and the like—that also use poetry.

Public Relations Writing: Articles and books may be spinoffs. If you are writing about topics of interest, see if that interest might go beyond the use for which you were hired. Often there are more options for such work than you realize.

Newspaper Writing: If you write freelance or full time for newspapers, see the articles section to determine other options for your work. Just keep in mind that if you are a staff employee for a paper or have been engaged on a "work for hire" basis under the 1976 Copyright Law, you will not be able to make a simultaneous submission without written permission from the publisher. You may do multiple marketing without a problem, however.

Six

KEEPING HOUSE

QUANTITY BUYING

Writing is a small business you conduct from home. This is the inescapable reality whether you have never sold, are selling occasionally, or are a full-time professional reading this book because you are less efficient than you should be. And like any small business, some of the greatest time-wasters are the endless chores you create for yourself by not having an adequate supply of tools available. There are certain items you will always use, always need. By anticipating them and buying accordingly, you can save yourself hours of time.

First there are the basics. What are you using to write? Do you make notes with a pen or pencil? If a pencil, be certain you have several, whether mechanical or wooden, with extra leads and erasers. If a pen, also have several, and additional refills.

Why should you have several pens or pencils? The reasons are obvious. First there is the intimidation factor. Pens and pencils are both arrogant and jealous of others. They like to feel that they are in power, in control of your life, and they become nervous when they are not. If you carry only one pen with you to an interview, a session at the library, or wherever else you will need it, it will break, run out of ink, and/or disappear before you arrive. It is in control. It can humiliate you even if there was, you thought, a fresh refill inside. However, let it know there is a spare available and it will work for months beyond what you thought was its capacity. It does not want to be upstaged or replaced. (I know this sounds silly. It is also unscientific. But if you have used pens as often as I have, you will know it is accurate.)

From a time management perspective, you cannot afford to have to go out constantly and replace items. When you are down to one or two pens, pencils, or refills, buy several more to have on hand.

The same is true with batteries if you do much tape recording of interviews. Buy several packages of batteries and carry spares with you. Ideally, buy rechargeable batteries with enough rechargers to handle at least three complete sets for your equipment. Carry at least two fully charged sets with you at all times, along with plug-in AC adapters so you do not have to use batteries at all unless you are away from a power outlet. Rechargeables last longer overall, but cannot be relied upon for more than two hours of continuous use when fully charged. (Count on ninety minutes to be safer.) Again, have more than you think you will need.

Interview tapes should also be purchased in quantity. The ultra-cheap variety often sold at three for a dollar in stores is a false economy for the professional writer. They've been known to jam or develop annoying hums at inopportune moments. The lowest priced versions of name brands (Sony, TDK, BASF, Memorex, etc.) generally are inexpensive in quantity. Buy twenty-five or more and most dealers will give you a substantial price break, also assuring that you will not run out. Depending upon how much taping you do, plan to buy additional tapes when you see that existing supplies will last for only the next three interviews. Many stores will give you a quantity discount, so shop around.

Typing paper should be purchased by the ream (five hundred sheets) if your writing volume is limited and by the case (ten reams) if your volume is heavy. Buy every time you see that you are down to only two weeks' supply. Be certain to shop around for this, though. You may find that the store that is the lowest price per ream is not the lowest price per case.

Envelopes are another item for quantity purchase. Generally, you will want four sizes: regular envelopes, the longer business size (#10), 9x12 envelopes for most manuscripts and manuscript returns (fold a second 9x12 in half after affixing postage and the address), and a lesser quantity of 10x13 envelopes for larger-than-normal manuscripts that will not fit in the 9x12 (remember that if the manuscript only fits in a 10x13 for mailing, you will need the same size envelope included for return. Some writers make the mistake of using a 10x13 for mailing, then enclosing a 9x12 for return). The small envelopes are sold in boxes of 100, the #10 envelopes in boxes of 50, and both are regularly put on sale by dime stores, drug stores, and discount houses. Larger quantities can be purchased from stationery and business supply stores. Shop around.

The price of larger envelopes will vary with the quantity and the supplier. There have been times when I have been able to purchase four 25-count packages of 9x12 envelopes for less money than a box of one hundred sold by the same store. Compare prices carefully because the differences can be substantial.

A postal scale is an important tool most writers overlook. If you have a moderately heavy-duty one (generally costing between $15 and $25), it will last for years and enable you to accurately weigh letters, manuscripts, and other items weighing up to five pounds.

Once you have a postage scale, get a copy of the current postal rates and update them regularly. Most writers are unfamiliar with manuscript rates or even first-class rates. They know the price for a one ounce stamp, then put the same amount for each additional ounce, not realizing that the price goes down for the second ounce. By having a scale and a rate sheet, you can buy stamps in whatever quantity your budget allows, keeping the denominations on hand that you will need. Instead of having to go to the post office every few days, you may be able to go every few weeks.

Other supplies you may need will include typewriter or printer ribbons, computer disks, and carbon paper for file copies. Even in this age of copiers, writers forget that making file copies with carbon paper is cheaper, easier, and less time-consuming than trying to locate a photocopy machine. A quality photocopy or additional printouts from a computer will only be necessary when additional originals are needed.

FILING IN AN ORDERLY MANNER

The more you work, the more swamped you seem to become. Clippings, information packets, notebooks, and other items relating to a variety of projects seem to be coming at you so rapidly that you never get ahead of them. For this reason it is important to get into a time-saving work habit of proper storage.

Establish the practice of daily filing and grouping your materials in a way that allows you to find everything quickly. This goes beyond the approaches discussed earlier.

You will find that your work falls into two categories— general areas of interest about which you write regularly and specific projects that may not relate to those areas. Each requires a separate approach to order so you do not waste time looking for things.

The preferred approach is to give your priority to specific projects. For example, I frequently write about true crime and regularly have extensive files about specific murder cases. These might include trial transcripts, correspondence, audiotapes, and copies of police documents, all related to one subject. I also have general reference materials related to crime, abnormal psychology, law enforcement investigation techniques, weapons, and so forth. Depending upon the book or article, I may or may not need to use these for background information.

The simplest approach I have found is to establish files for each project, breaking them down by large groupings. Trial transcripts are obvious, but I will have a file for general correspondence where appropriate, then files related to aspects of the person's life and case. One file might contain newspaper and/or magazine clips while another might include information relating to the city, business, or other location where the crime took place. Additional files on the case might relate to the victim, to periods in the life of the killer, and so on. If I have to do extensive interviews, I may file the transcriptions by the name of the subject or I may file several together if they all relate to a specific period of time.

With a biography, I try to break down the files according to sections of the person's life. Transcriptions of interviews usually show that the subject rambled over several years. I clip the pages and file them in a logical order so that when I am ready to write, I do not have to find tapes 15, 17, and 23 in order to write about the person's high school days. I can just go to the high school folder and know that all the relevant transcription pages have been placed there.

By contrast, columnist and author Leon Lindheim only writes about the field of numismatics. His files all relate to coin history, the subjects broken down by types of coin, country, mint, etc. When a question arises for research, the topic of the question will correspond to one or more of his files which are updated as new material comes in or is clipped from hobby and scholarly publications.

Try to keep the work grouped in logical ways for the

writing you do. For example, for several years I wrote articles and "ghosted" books on American artists. At first I tried storing them alphabetically. Then I realized that I was often writing about artists who lived and worked in the same geographical area. I switched my files so that they were grouped in this manner. As a result, when I was asked to write a book about the artists of Taos, New Mexico, I did not have to research who they were. I opened a file drawer containing nothing but Taos artists and could just take out the stack of folders and go to work.

How you group your information will depend upon your needs. Just be certain your approach is logical for you and that you complete your filing each day. As someone who is regularly surrounded by heaping stacks of papers, I can vouch for the fact that without such order, trying to find even last week's work would take precious hours.

ESTABLISHING YOUR TERRITORY

Comedian Rodney Dangerfield has established an image of a man who gets no respect. Writers are the same way. Unless you establish your territory, your scissors will disappear into the basement, your typing paper will become a child artist's drawing paper or the family notepad, and other essentials will also seem to vanish. You get no respect.

The ideal situation is to convert an area that can be closed off into your basic office. Earlier I mentioned writer Sue Downey's converted closet, a rather frustrating space but still one that was hers alone.

Some writers who must work in their living rooms use a cabinet-style piece of furniture ("The Organizer" is the name of one brand but there are several companies manufacturing variations) that can be closed and locked with the essentials inside. It opens to reveal a desk work area, file cabinet, shelving, and other essentials which will hold all the basics, including reference books. Others have been known to buy an inexpensive folding screen that can be erected to serve as a wall of sorts. Whatever the case, it is important that the area you stake out be as inviolate as an office you can close and lock.

One word of caution: Since creating such a space requires family cooperation when you do not have a separate room of your own, be certain you do not establish a bad precedent by your own actions. The dictionary, thesaurus, other reference works, pens, and other supplies that you use should never be given to spouse or children. You may buy matching reference works, one set for the family, the other for your office, but you need to ensure that your things are respected.

FILE CABINETS AND OTHER FORMS OF STORAGE

File cabinets are critical for your work. There are essentially three types you may need and each has its place. The first type is the ultra-cheap variety sold by many discount stores, the type that lacks full suspension. This means that if the greatest weight is in the top drawer, when you pull out the drawer, the entire cabinet may start to fall forward.

Next comes the full suspension cabinet, more expensive, but with better construction and balance. A top-heavy file drawer of this type is not likely to tilt over.

Finally there are the fire-resistant file drawers. These are extremely expensive and range from full four-drawer models to units that have one to three regular drawers and a single fire-resistant drawer. The least expensive have a ten-year life. The most expensive will always be fire resistant. Either way, you only need them when your work includes confidential and/or irreplaceable materials.

NOTE: Fire-resistant file drawers are designed to prevent damage to paper. The temperatures paper can withstand before bursting into flames are higher than the temperatures computer disks can tolerate before being damaged. If you want to provide adequate home protection for computer disks, you will need to buy a more expensive unit specifically designed for this end.

Check several office supply places for prices on all this equipment. You will find that identical units by different manufacturers will vary in price from a few dollars (regular suspension units) to several hundred dollars (fire-resistant four-drawer units).

Some writers create their own desks or additional work area with filing cabinets. They purchase a flat wooden door, either fully finished or unfinished, and place it on top of from two to four of the least expensive two-drawer file cabinets they can find. The weight of the door acts as a counterbalance to the file cabinets and they have a desk or extended work area, as they choose, for far less than the cost of a regular desk.

Be certain your filing cabinets have locks if you have curious children. These locks are not meant for security. They are meant for privacy. Many writers have discovered important papers with their backs "decorated" by curious explorers wielding crayons. The simple locks are more than adequate until the children fully understand your need for privacy.

COMPUTERS

If you do not currently own a computer or word processor, this should be a priority purchase as soon as you can afford it. Computers and word processors are the greatest time-savers ever devised for writers.

Never mind all the things you keep hearing computers can accomplish, such as graphic design, business programs, and the like. Chances are you will never do anything but utilize them as glorified typewriters. Even the least expensive machine is likely to have capabilities beyond anything you will ever try to learn.

So why am I so enthusiastic?

Editing. When I used a typewriter, I would write a manuscript, then sit down and make corrections between the lines. Next I would return to the typewriter and make my next draft. Then I would examine it and make changes. This would continue until the work was the best of which I was capable or, more likely, until I got sick of writing endless drafts.

The problems were magnified with each book. If I decided that page 27 needed major revisions, I might have to re-type three hundred pages before I could submit the manuscript because everything was off. Adding little inserts throughout (Page 27A, for example) was possible, but the work did not look professional. I also could turn the work over to a professional typist, buying me several additional hours to work on new material, but also adding the typist's charge to the as-yet-unsold project.

I don't have to worry about these problems with a computer. Is there a problem on page 27? I fix it, even if my numbering is off. The computer renumbers for me.

Do I want to shift paragraphs? Restructure chapters? Move sentences about? Two or three strokes on the keyboard and it's done automatically.

Is Chapter 3 going so badly that even individual sentences are being reworked a dozen times? That's okay. I can cope with it. I simply make the changes on the screen. I don't tell the machine to type out my manuscript until it is the best I feel it can be in the time available. Then it is typed out only once, at a speed much faster than work done by hand.

The reality of the computer is that I literally tripled my output when I made the switch. The writing still takes as long. The research is still just as involved. The words come no faster and require no fewer rewrites. But in the course of a year, I am not needlessly retyping hundreds of pages of material that was good except for a few minor changes that threw off my original pagination.

There are essentially four types of computers on the market today. There is the standard desktop computer with which you are probably familiar, the portable, the laptop, and the laptop with interchangeable screens. The portable means anything with a handle attached. There are systems weighing as little as seven pounds at this writing, all the way to those weighing approximately thirty-five pounds.

A laptop is a portable that is small, has a built-in screen, and runs on both batteries and AC. The difference between the two types of laptops is that some have a removable screen that can be replaced by a standard monitor when you're using it at your desk.

There are also what are known as dedicated word processors that cost the same as midpriced electric and electronic typewriters. Most of these contain their own printers and are little different in appearance from the old office manual machines. A word processor essentially is a typewriter with all the editing functions of a computer but which can do little or nothing more. Disk storage is available but the disks are currently not compatible with IBM or Apple machines, the industry standards.

As a writer, you're probably best served by a laptop with replaceable monitor if you can afford it. The unit can be carried anywhere in a briefcase or its own holder, it can be used anywhere so long as you keep the batteries charged, costs less to operate than a full-sized computer, and will use the same word processing programs designed for larger machines. A good laptop will do everything you would ever want a standard machine to do and it will do it anywhere. Mine has been used in airports, hotel rooms, and equally unlikely areas, often gaining me hours of productive time.

NOTE: Laptop screens vary. Try different models to be certain you can comfortably read off a particular model, without eyestrain. All such units are well built today and will do everything you need with limited maintenance over time. Buy according to comfort and price.

Printers are a second concern, including the printers that come with dedicated word processors. There are several types you will hear about. Daisy wheel, dot matrix, 24-pin, laser, and thermal are most common.

A daisy wheel printer is nothing more than a typewriter triggered by the machine. Most electronic typewriters use daisy wheels. The print quality is perfect for your needs and the only drawback is that they are slower than some of the other units. However, they are simple, sturdy, and generally offer few problems.

A standard dot matrix machine should *not* be purchased.

The quality of the printing will work against your freelance efforts. In fact, there are publishers and television script readers who have told me that they automatically refuse to look at dot matrix submissions.

Why this problem? A dot matrix printer creates letters by laying a pattern of dots on the paper. You have the illusion of full letters and that illusion is easy to read—when you are fresh and just starting the day. Once your eyes become tired, you tend to see dot matrix writing for what it is, dots swimming before your eyes. Editors, publishers, script readers, and the like spend a large portion of their time reading. By the end of their work days, dot matrix printing is so difficult to read that they often will reject it out of hand. It may not be fair, but knowing this reality, you must not purchase a standard dot matrix printer, including those that say they offer "near letter quality." It is either letter quality, meaning it looks typewritten, or it is not.

A 24-pin printer is a dot matrix printer with a difference. Many of them offer true letter quality by putting down so many dots per letter that there is enough ink to fill all the spaces. Many will offer a draft mode (dot matrix) and letter quality mode, a much slower version where enough additional dots per letter are placed on the paper to fill in all the spaces. Not all 24-pin printers offer true letter quality, though most do. Look at the results before buying.

A laser printer is a high-speed device that uses ink jets. At this writing it is too expensive for most writers. However, prices are coming down and it can print a letter quality page in a few seconds compared with up to 2½ minutes for the slowest of the daisy wheel units.

Thermal printers are to be avoided entirely. The results are a little like unfixed photographs. No matter how good they look, over time and with exposure to heat and light, the pages will darken. They may cause you problems short term, but they will always cause you problems long term.

Computer "software" means the programs available for the computer. These are the items that tell the computer what to do and there are many available for writers. Among the features to consider (all have basic editing abilities) are spelling checks, indexing, and the ability to take a list of addresses, then add them to form letters to make as many identical queries, each properly addressed to a different person and company, as you may need.

There are numerous programs for home bookkeeping and other functions and you may be the rare individual who actually uses them. Most writers find that when they are not using their computer for word processing (writing), they are not using it. You can balance your checkbook faster and easier with an inexpensive pocket calculator. File cards make for better recipe storage. And buying computer games represents just another excuse to avoid writing.

FAMILY INVOLVEMENT IN WRITING

One of the problems with being a writer at home is that you present an odd contradiction. You are in the midst of others yet you are demanding privacy. If you have small children, this is even more frustrating for them. They cannot understand what you are trying to do, they may feel neglected, or they may wish to be involved, a reality that can prove to be a nuisance.

Childhood perceptions are especially difficult. For example, I know one writer who was extremely excited when he finally was selling well enough to quit his job and work from home. A large extra bedroom became his office where he would go each morning, working eight to ten hours per day, delighting in having achieved every writer's goal of independence. The happiness dissolved when his child came home from school in tears.

According to the child, the teacher asked the children what their parents did for a living. His child had been ridiculed because her father did nothing. He did not go to work. He just stayed home.

Obviously the child was too young to comprehend the

life of the freelance writer and the success required to be able to "not go to work" each day. The only solution was for the writer to arise each day, put on a suit, leave the house, buy the morning paper, and sit on a bench, well away from the direction the child took to school. He read until just after the child left, then returned home to write. He lost some time, but his child now understood that her father had a real job like everyone else.

A better system is to involve the family any way you can. Small children make great envelope stuffers and stamp lickers. (Make certain they are old enough to be responsible and careful, though.) At certain ages they make excellent proofreaders and typists.

Smaller children can sharpen pencils, clip articles you need to have saved, and handle other simple tasks. Older children who have just earned their driver's licenses will delight in running all those chores you need to have done, provided they have use of the family car.

You might also be able to hire children to handle those chores you would normally do yourself around the house. Shoveling snow, cutting grass, raking leaves, and similar tasks that take time from your writing can be exciting to a child old enough to understand the value of money and able to handle the work.

Spouses can be enlisted for certain types of researching in libraries and other resources. They know that they are keeping you from being distracted, yet they often delight in the knowledge that they are doing something practical for your career. They feel they are helping in the one area where they can be of assistance. Such involvement thus works well for everyone.

Admittedly this seems a little manipulative on your part for, certainly, the writer gains the benefits. However, you will find that family members often have a need to feel as though they can be a part of your new career efforts. Their actions free your time, provide genuine assistance, and may make them happy. You all benefit to some degree.

OTHER FORMS OF FAMILY HARMONY

No book about time management for writers would be complete without mentioning some emotional realities. Writing is an extraordinary solitary profession. Writers must be completely withdrawn into themselves when they work. Our production depends upon our living inside of our heads, an action totally opposite the natural socialization that is a part of being human.

Some writers are natural loners. For many, the isolation is a small price to pay for the joy of being a writer. If they are naturally rather gregarious, they put this tendency on "hold" during the hours they work.

A frequent problem is that we are working when others think that we are not. One particular day I was sitting with my wife, trying to develop a plot twist, while she read a book. For more than an hour I developed what would happen and how the characters would handle the problem. Then, finished, I turned to Leslie and said, "Let's do something together. I've missed you."

Surprised, she said, "But we've been together for an hour."

"You were physically near me for that time," I explained. "But I was 2,000 miles away in the city where Donna and Liz are working to resolve a murder case. I was totally unaware of your presence."

Fortunately Leslie understood what I meant. Equally fortunate was the fact that I learned, after a failed first marriage, to make the effort to be a human being.

The reality is that writing is not the most important part of our lives. It may be one of our greatest pleasures, but unless we take the time to also enjoy friends and family, it can take on an undue importance that destroys everything else. No matter how limited your writing time, set aside regular periods for others, meeting their needs as well as your own.

Also recognize that there will be interruptions. Family members will get sick and need your attention. A child may be lead snowflake in the Christmas pageant at school. Respect the important moments in their lives and be flexible about your work. You will be a better writer if you maintain the life-style of a whole person than if you let your approach to time management destroy your relations with all else you hold dear.

Afterword

Because I teach writing on a part-time basis, I am often asked by new students if I think that they have talent. I always explain that I don't know what talent is. The best natural writer I ever saw lacked the drive to do the rewriting, the extra step needed to go from "almost right" to an excellent draft. The worst writer I ever taught, one who had to complete six drafts before reaching the level other students reached the first time they tried, eventually became a full-time professional. He had the drive to keep working.

The reality is that writing is a growth skill. The more you do, the better you become. Every time I write a book, it is the best of which I am capable or I have failed my reader. At the same time, because I am constantly striving to improve, it is also hopefully better than my last. I am only as good as my next work. I know that even a book I wrote six months ago, perhaps one that was on a bestseller list, could easily be improved today. Certainly you could read my books or those of any other writer and see all manner of ways to improve them.

The result of this reality is that no matter where your current skill level, there is no such thing as a wasted writing effort. Thus the better you manage your time, the more writing you will accomplish and the faster your skills will improve.

Now review this book again, focusing on those sections which most apply to you. Keep your writing in perspective but work to ensure that every available moment can be utilized to the fullest, whether you are just beginning or have already begun making regular sales. Effective time management is one major key to professional success in the field we both love so dearly.

Index

Other Books of Interest

General Writing Books
  Beginning Writer's Answer Book, edited by Kirk Polking (paper) $12.95
  Beyond Style: Mastering the Finer Points of Writing, by Gary Provost $14.95
  Getting the Words Right: How to Revise, Edit and Rewrite, by Theodore A. Rees Cheney $14.95
  How to Get Started in Writing, by Peggy Teeters (paper) $9.95
  How to Increase Your Word Power, by the editors of Reader's Digest $19.95
  How to Write a Book Proposal, by Michael Larsen $9.95
  How to Write While You Sleep, by Elizabeth Ross $14.95
  Just Open a Vein, edited by William Brohaugh $15.95
  Knowing Where to Look: The Ultimate Guide to Research, by Lois Horowitz $18.95
  Make Every Word Count, by Gary Provost (paper) $7.95
  Pinckert's Practical Grammar, by Robert C. Pinckert $14.95
  The 29 Most Common Writing Mistakes & How to Avoid Them, by Judy Delton $9.95
  Writer's Block & How to Use It, by Victoria Nelson $14.95
  The Writer's Digest Guide to Manuscript Formats, by Buchman & Groves $16.95
  Writer's Encyclopedia, edited by Kirk Polking (paper) $16.95
  Writer's Market, edited by Glenda Neff $21.95
  Writing for the Joy of It, by Leonard Knott $11.95

Nonfiction Writing
  Basic Magazine Writing, by Barbara Kevles $16.95
  How to Sell Every Magazine Article You Write, by Lisa Collier Cool $14.95
  Writing Creative Nonfiction, by Theodore A. Rees Cheney $15.95
  Writing Nonfiction that Sells, by Samm Sinclair Baker $14.95

Fiction Writing
  Creating Short Fiction, by Damon Knight (paper) $8.95
  Dare to Be a Great Writer: 329 Keys to Powerful Fiction, by Leonard Bishop $15.95
  Fiction is Folks: How to Create Unforgettable Characters, by Robert Newton Peck (paper) $8.95
  Fiction Writer's Market, edited by Laurie Henry $19.95
  Handbook of Short Story Writing: Vol. I, by Dickson and Smythe (paper) $8.95
  Handbook of Short Story Writing: Vol. II, edited by Jean M. Fredette $15.95
  How to Write & Sell Your First Novel, by Oscar Collier with Frances Spatz Leighton $15.95
  Storycrafting, by Paul Darcy Boles (paper) $9.95
  Writing the Novel: From Plot to Print, by Lawrence Block (paper) $8.95

Special Interest Writing Books
  The Children's Picture Book: How to Write It, How to Sell It, by Ellen E.M. Roberts (paper) $15.95
  Comedy Writing Secrets, by Melvin Helitzer $16.95
  The Complete Book of Scriptwriting, by J. Michael Straczynski (paper) $9.95
  The Craft of Lyric Writing, by Sheila Davis $18.95
  Editing Your Newsletter, by Mark Beach (paper) $18.50
  Guide to Greeting Card Writing, edited by Larry Sandman (paper) $8.95
  How to Make Money Writing About Fitness & Health, by Celia & Thomas Scully $16.95

How to Sell & Re-Sell Your Writing, by Duane Newcomb $10.95
How to Write a Play, by Raymond Hull (paper) $10.95
How to Write & Sell A Column, by Raskin & Males $10.95
How to Write and Sell Your Personal Experiences, by Lois Duncan (paper) $9.95
How to Write and Sell (Your Sense of) Humor, by Gene Perret (paper) $9.95
How to Write Tales of Horror, Fantasy & Science Fiction, edited by J.N. Williamson $15.95
How to Write the Story of Your Life, by Frank P. Thomas $14.95
How You Can Make $50,000 a Year as a Nature Photojournalist, by Bill Thomas (paper) $17.95
Mystery Writer's Handbook, by The Mystery Writers of America (paper) $9.95
Nonfiction for Children: How to Write It, How to Sell It, by Ellen E.M. Roberts $16.95
The Poet's Handbook, by Judson Jerome (paper) $9.95
Poet's Market, by Judson Jerome $17.95
Travel Writer's Handbook, by Louise Zobel (paper) $11.95
TV Scriptwriter's Handbook, by Alfred Brenner (paper) $9.95
Writing for Children & Teenagers, by Lee Wyndham (paper) $9.95
Writing Short Stories for Young People, by George Edward Stanley $15.95
Writing the Modern Mystery, by Barbara Norville $15.95
Writing to Inspire, edited by William Gentz (paper) $14.95
Writing Young Adult Novels, by Hadley Irwin & Jeanette Eyerly $14.95

The Writing Business

A Beginner's Guide to Getting Published, edited by Kirk Polking $10.95
Complete Guide to Self-Publishing, by Tom & Marilyn Ross $19.95
How to Bulletproof Your Manuscript, by Bruce Henderson $9.95
How to Understand and Negotiate a Book Contract or Magazine Agreement, by Richard Balkin $11.95
How to Write Irresistible Query Letters, by Lisa Collier Cool $10.95
How to Write with a Collaborator, by Hal Bennett with Michael Larsen $11.95
How You Can Make $25,000 a Year Writing (No Matter Where You Live), by Nancy Edmonds Hanson $15.95
Literary Agents: How to Get & Work with the Right One for You, by Michael Larsen $9.95
Professional Etiquette for Writers, by William Brohaugh $9.95

To order directly from the publisher, include $2.00 postage and handling for 1 book and 50¢ for each additional book. Allow 30 days for delivery.

Writer's Digest Books
1507 Dana Avenue, Cincinnati, Ohio 45207
Credit card orders call TOLL-FREE
1-800-543-4644 (Outside Ohio)
1-800-551-0884 (Ohio only)
Prices subject to change without notice.

Write to this same address for information on *Writer's Digest* magazine, Writer's Digest Book Club, Writer's Digest School, and Writer's Digest Criticism Service.